MAKE IT WORK

22 Time-Tested, Real-Life Lessons for Sustaining a Healthy, Happy Relationship

TONY A. GASKINS JR.

HOWARD BOOKS

New York   London   Toronto   Sydney   New Delhi

HOWARD
BOOKS

An Imprint of Simon & Schuster, Inc.
1230 Avenue of the Americas
New York, NY 10020

First Howard Books hardcover edition January 2019

HOWARD and colophon are trademarks of Simon & Schuster, Inc.

For information about special discounts for bulk purchases,
please contact Simon & Schuster Special Sales at 1-866-506-1949
or business@simonandschuster.com.

The Simon & Schuster Speakers Bureau can bring authors to your live event.
For more information or to book an event, contact the Simon & Schuster Speakers Bureau
at 1-866-248-3049 or visit our website at www.simonspeakers.com.

Interior design by Davina Mock-Maniscalco

Manufactured in the United States of America

10   9   8   7   6   5   4   3

Library of Congress Cataloging-in-Publication Data

Names: Gaskins, Tony A., author.
Title: Make it work : 22 time-tested, real-life lessons for sustaining a healthy, happy relationship / Tony A. Gaskins Jr.
Description: New York : Howard Books, [2019]
Identifiers: LCCN 2018028708 (print) | LCCN 2018031673 (ebook) | ISBN 9781501199349 (E-book) | ISBN 9781501199325 (hardcover) | ISBN 9781501199332 (pbk.)
Subjects: LCSH: Man-woman relationships. | Couples. | Interpersonal relations. | Interpersonal conflict.
Classification: LCC HQ801 (ebook) | LCC HQ801 .G355 2019 (print) | DDC 306.7—dc23
LC record available at https://lccn.loc.gov/2018028708.

ISBN 978-1-5011-9932-5
ISBN 978-1-5011-9934-9 (ebook)

If you don't learn how to love, someone will teach you how to hate.
Then you'll confuse the two.

contents

introduction

Love is the greatest wonder of the world. For thousands of years we have tried to figure it out, but still we struggle to make it work. I became a student of love early in life. I had my first girlfriend in kindergarten, although I'm not sure that counts. As early as tenth grade, I can recall conducting three-way phone calls with two girls who needed advice about their boyfriends. As I grew into young adulthood, I went on to make every mistake a man can make in love. I was the worst boyfriend a girl could find but wrapped in the best package. I was a nightmare disguised as a dream. I said all the right things and had the résumé to match. It didn't hurt that I wasn't the ugliest guy on the block, either. I was lost, confused, and trying to figure out love. I broke hearts, and I had my heart broken. By the age of twenty-two, I'd already dated over a hundred ladies, and I'd kept very good notes. I turned all my mistakes into lessons. I allowed my pain to birth my purpose. My mess became my message. I decided to use my story for God's glory. At twenty-three years old, I married the love of my life. A month later, our first son was born. Two months after that, I was robbed of my car, which was my most prized possession. That sent me to my knees, and I questioned the decisions I'd made up until that point. It's crazy how the loss of a material possession can shake a man to his core. I decided to rededicate my life to Christ, and began living with my Christian values again. The first two years of marriage were the most challenging, and I admit I made some mistakes. By the end of the first two years of marriage, I got my act together. I began sharing my lessons online, and the tweets started going viral. Then I went to Facebook. Then I expanded to Instagram. Millions of people hit the "follow" or "like" buttons on my posts. I realized then that my mistakes weren't in vain. Christ is a redeemer. My story is proof of that. They say certain types of people can't change; well, I'm one of those people who truly changed.

I'll never refer to myself as a guru or an expert. Although many have labeled me as such, I choose to call myself a servant. There are people who once knew me and women I once dated who can't believe the man I am today. They cannot believe my transformation is real, but it is. Had I not changed, I wouldn't be writing this book today.

I began writing books at the age of twenty-two. I prayed and asked God to double my wisdom every day. I prayed for strength, grace, mercy, and favor. I knew He gave me a simple message about love that human nature tends to complicate. Sharing my message online began to open up to a new world full of opportunities. People began to ask me to speak at their events. They had never heard me speak and didn't know if I had the ability or charisma to carry a stage, but they invited me anyway. I was invited to speak at various events ranging from church retreats and high schools to seminars for professional athletes. The NBA called me in to speak to the rookie classes, and an NFL team called me to speak to their athletes. I spoke on toxic relationships and the concept of becoming a man. Women's groups began inviting me to their events to serve as the male voice. Based on my online work, they could tell I didn't pull any punches but that my aim was to help and serve. You see, I played the game at a high level and I did a lot of dirt. You can't truly have a life-changing message unless you've had life-changing circumstances.

Then I received requests from around the world. It started with Johannesburg, South Africa. I spoke to one crowd of 2,000 and another crowd of more than 5,000. Johannesburg featured me on every media outlet, and millions of people saw my face or heard my voice. More than 100,000 people in Africa joined my social media following.

I was called to speak on two other continents and in more than ten countries. I was only thirty years old. Top celebrities, entertainers, and professional athletes began to reach out to me. High-profile figures flew me in to their homes to ask for my insight into personal relationship issues. Before long, television networks began calling me to appear on program episodes as a life coach. Many production companies have been trying to find the right show for me, but I'm patient because the message has to be packaged just right. In our world, the truth as I tell it isn't always popular. I'm compelled to share it because it changed my life and the lives of thousands of others.

At the age of thirty-one, I was called to be the life coach for an NBA team. This was after occupying that role for several Division I college teams. I didn't ask for the opportunities; they found me while I was in the "fields" working. I can't say I was always ready; the organizations had never utilized life coaches prior to my involvement, so they were unsure of my role. Truthfully, I wasn't completely sure myself. God and I created a blueprint for the space. I made mistakes, and I learned from them. I've dedicated my life to teaching as I learn. Tomorrow is not promised to any of us, so I teach daily. If it has helped me, I know it can help someone else. It's my work to share what I've learned.

My life experience is the tool I am using to write this book. I'm not a counselor or a therapist. The books they study to become certified are based on lives like the one I lived firsthand. I was never the top of my class in school, so I earned my PhD from Mistakes University. I began to notice how many people preferred a truth from life experience rather than hearing the lessons learned from a textbook. So in addition to the counselors and therapists, people came to me for insight. It wasn't long before I was overwhelmed. Even today, I have more than 10,000 unread messages asking for advice sitting in my inbox. I learned very quickly that I had to share the lessons I learned in ways that could reach great masses of people at once. I coached thousands of people one-on-one. At the age of twenty-seven, I had to resign from my job as a group home counselor to become a full-time author, coach, and motivational speaker.

I read as many messages as I can. I speak to as many people as I can. I put my finger on the pulse of the people, and I learn lessons from thousands of stories each year. The average therapist speaks with around ten to twenty clients per week. I was interacting with one hundred to four hundred through social media and email. For an eight- to twelve-hour workday, I read emails. The emails were stories from people ages sixteen to sixty-eight from more than eighty countries. I was thrust into the belly of the beast. I'd be willing to bet that I have one of the top ten relationship data mines in the world. At the peak of my Facebook popularity, my page reached between 20 million and 40 million people per week without my paying to boost a single post. That reach allowed me to gather more data and insight than any scientist in a lab. These were real lives, real stories, real pain, and real experiences. I have read things that would make you faint and not wake up for a week. I have read relationship stories that would make a rock cry. Yes, it gets that real. If life allows me, I'll write seventy more books tackling different aspects of love and relationships, because it gets that real.

Please understand that the words on these pages are not just my opinion snatched out of thin air. This all stems from findings, insight, and the wisdom I've gained over more than twelve years of intensely studying relationships and the dynamics of love, not just in America but also all around the world. I've heard more stories and coached more relationships than I can count. This book will scratch the surface of the knowledge I've acquired, but I believe it will confirm or reveal to you some key lessons for making a relationship work.

When I write and when I speak, I am not alone. I'm just a vessel. I'm just sharing the message that has been given to me to share. Take it for what it's worth, and in due season it will bless you where you need it to.

one

YOU DON'T KNOW LOVE

Think about when you learned how to love. All human beings are born with the ability to love, but love is a learned behavior. Most people learn how to love by the examples around them. In most cases, people first learn from their parents. Many people were raised in single-parent homes, so the love between two adults in an intimate manner was not often displayed. Others were raised in two-parent homes. In half of those homes, the love was toxic, so the wrong way to love was passed down. In the other half of those homes, the parents hid their problems, so the kids watching mistakenly believed that all relationships are perfect. Very rarely do people learn how to love correctly. Not many can say they saw healthy love between their biological parents or got to see how they effectively handled disagreements. Although you may be one of those people who received healthy exposure, you most likely will date or marry someone who cannot say the same. The fact that it takes two to make it work means there will always be a 50 percent chance that unhealthy modeling could negatively affect your relationship. I've made many observations over the years, and I have discovered some interesting things. These aren't diagnoses—just observations. I can't speak for everyone but I believe the lessons I've learned over the last decade as a relationship coach can be applied to many relationships.

In the biological two-parent home like the one I grew up in, the climate can be healthy, yet it can also be confusing. My parents were grade school sweethearts who stuck it out together and finally got married. When I was born, my mother was twenty years old and my dad was twenty-one. Both of my parents were the youngest of twelve siblings. In a sense, they raised themselves. Yes, they had parental input, but that can be challenging in a home with only two children, so imagine a family unit of twelve children.

My parents saw a lot of ups and downs throughout their childhood, so much so that they don't really talk about it. Once I was older, I could clearly see dysfunction that stemmed from their childhood. My maternal grandmother told me stories of throwing boiling water on one man and biting another man's finger off. I saw aunts with broken bones, busted lips, and black eyes. Love was definitely synonymous with pain.

Those things made my mother a little fireball. She wasn't the submissive type. She was a fighter. She stood her ground and spoke her mind. She loved hard, but she loved wrong. At a young age, my father lost his mother. She was killed by gunshot. My father has never really discussed the details of that story. I feel like I still see the pain in his eyes. On my dad's side of the family, I see a number of long-term relationships. But I see silent pain. I see strong, domineering men with quiet and submissive women. So naturally, my dad grew up with the "my way or the highway" mentality and wanted to be the head of his household. Maintaining that mentality is tough for any man to do when he marries a fireball. The most toxic interactions between my parents occurred before I was six years old. After that I didn't really see my dad arguing anymore. It felt like he was serving a sentence, holding on just to be present for his children. My mother would put up a fuss and fight, and my dad would become gentler in front of us. I believe a lot of it was due to my dad becoming ordained as a preacher. I could see that both my parents were trying to grow. They were so close that their relationship was more like a relationship between siblings or friends rather than a relationship between husband and wife. My mother openly disagreed with my father on biblical concepts, but she would object in front of the entire church during Bible study. That's not something most wives would do.

My parents lacked a real marital structure. Of course, if you let them tell it, I'm 100 percent wrong and what I saw didn't really happen. But that's the problem with perception; we get from it what we want, and that may not always be what it was. I was decoding love all around me, not just in my home, and those childhood lessons taught me that a man is the head of the household and he is supposed to lead and dominate. Those same lessons taught me that the woman is supposed to submit and be quiet. If she does not submit and if she is not quiet, she isn't fit for the role of a wife and she must be either put into her place or let go.

As an adult I learned that this mind-set was completely wrong, but the truth remains that it was what life initially taught me about relationships and marriage. It was the most common type of relationship dynamic I saw as a child. On the other hand, I saw men who would give up on trying to lead because their women were just too headstrong. Those men would remain quiet and reserved, and the women would call all the shots. Relationships looked like *The Hunger Games*. They began to look like survival of the fittest. Whoever had the toughest childhood and had built the thickest skin, that's who would win in this war of love. As children growing up, how are we supposed to read all of these messages?

Then I saw biological two-parent homes that were seemingly perfect. The parents never argued in front of their children. These relationships appeared to be fifty-fifty, and somehow, no matter what the decision was to be made, the parents just magically came to the same decision at the same time. It was an odd thing to see. The problem was, "they had holes in their socks." In other words, you just couldn't see their problems. They would fight and argue behind a closed bedroom door when the kids were asleep. Or one person in the marriage had given up his or her true identity and had become a shell of him- or herself. Just writing this is scaring me to death, thinking about what my very intuitive son could be reading from his mother and me. We learn in a very special way, and none of what we pick up comes with a user's manual. We are deciphering everything as it happens in real time, and it's shaping how we view the world. We learn to love ourselves or hate ourselves; love others or hate others. We learn as we go. A "perfect" home can produce kids who later enter relationships and find themselves shocked and ill-prepared when arguments arise. They won't know how to handle it. They might run, cry, give up, or become victims. If they have never seen marital conflict solved, they will have no clue how to bring about solutions. I have noticed that my clients from those types of homes sometimes struggle the most. They lose themselves in relationships and experience a great deal of pain because the reality of a relationship is much different from the fairy tale they had in mind. They quickly lose hope in finding what their parents displayed, so they settle for what's in front of them.

No matter what our backgrounds are, we all rack up our fair share of skeletons in our closets. There are a lot of things being swept under the rug that we eventually trip over down the line. There are a lot of misconceptions about love. As the famous quote says, "We don't see things for what they are; we see them for what we are."

I've also seen some results of single-parent homes. In one home, there is usually a strong single parent who never dates in front of their child. They are so protective of the child that the child never sees an intimate relationship play out. The parent may be sexually active and may have a partner, but the child doesn't know it. Because the parent is guarding the child so much, he or she can't fully develop a real relationship with another adult, so every relationship fizzles out. Children in this type of family thus grow up seeing independence, or so they think. They see the parent doing it all alone, so it shapes their mind into believing that you can't depend on love. You can't depend on humans. You can depend on God and yourself—that's it. These children are taught to get their coins and take care of home. They most often grow up to be very strong-minded and independent. Some are able to attract love, but the others struggle with making love work because they can't seem to figure out how to go from independent to interdependent. Many who do get married may still find themselves being very independent even in marriage. Allowing someone to help them may be difficult. Asking a partner for help may be even harder. Too much independence eventually breaks a relationship down, but because single life was the only exposure they saw, they almost feel most comfortable being alone. Again, this is in some cases, not all.

Then there is the single parent who dates around. Children with this kind of parent grow up believing that love is an illusion. They don't believe in real love. They believe in getting all you can get from a relationship and then moving on. It's okay to love and lose. It's okay to have soul ties. Although many can break the cycle, there are many who can't. No matter who we are, it's often difficult to admit that what we saw had an effect on us. We want to believe that we each are our own person and that nothing has affected us. But that's usually just a lie we're telling ourselves.

Then there are the stepparent homes. Those homes can be stable, sometimes more stable than the biological parent homes. Many times, the child gets a false reality about parental love. The reason is because stepparents spend every waking moment trying to earn the love of the stepchild. The stepchild perceives that as the standard for how he or she is supposed to be treated and may fail to realize that not everything will go their way in love or in parenting. Subconsciously, some of these children are taught that divorce is a part of life and that if things get too hard, you just need to hit the restart button. In some cases, that may be necessary, but it all depends on how the child perceived what they saw. Some enter marriage with divorce as an option. They are quietly saying to themselves, *The moment I'm not happy, I'm leaving, and my next spouse will love my kids like their own.* We often don't think about the power in those subconscious messages we are speaking to ourselves.

We really have to question the source. We have to learn what real love is, what it looks like, what it feels like, and what it sounds like. Then we have to compare that to what we know to be true. We have to be honest with ourselves. It's one of the hardest things we'll ever do. There are times a thought comes to mind, and I have to stop that thought and address it immediately. I have to say to myself, *That's not love. That's what you picked up along the way from someone who didn't know how to love.* Addressing these thoughts is a daily battle you must aim to win.

If we are not careful, what we were once exposed to is exactly what we will become. I was involved in a toxic relationship during my college years. All the pain and dysfunction I saw around me growing up had programmed me, and I didn't know what it meant to be a real man. I was a grown-boy. My girlfriend had been programmed as well, and she had no idea what it meant to be loved. We both came from biological two-parent homes. You'd think that would have made us a great fit for each other. That was the most toxic relationship I'd ever experienced. She saw abuse in her home in different forms. I saw abuse in my home in different forms. Not all abuse is physical. I'd never seen my dad hit my mom or my mom hit my dad, but I witnessed the yelling, screaming, and arguing. I saw both of them playing mind games against each other. Abuse is a strong word, but it's the word I need to use so that it's taken seriously enough. My ex saw her mother being physically abused and then saw her sisters suffer abuse at the hands of their boyfriends. She told me that if it's not that type of love, it's not love. She thought that in order for a relationship to be real, the man has to care enough about it to hit the woman. So reaching that level of abuse was her goal. I didn't realize it until my sister brought it to my attention. I was floored.

They say hindsight is 20/20, so in retrospect, it all made sense to me. I was young and trying to love but didn't know the definition of love. It was a recipe for disaster because I thought being a man meant being in control, and she thought being a woman meant being controlled but the control had to pass a certain threshold of pain. The relationship was draining. I was tired of arguing and going back and forth. I was tired of playing detective with each other. Looking back, I can see how our upbringings shaped us. It wasn't just our home lives; it was the everyday things we saw around us as well. I ended the relationship because I was tired. Although I was trying to be in control, I felt controlled. I felt weak. I felt manipulated. I felt like I was under emotional abuse that was leading me to want to reciprocate. Although I didn't fully know love, I knew that what I had with her was not it.

I urge you to question your teachers of love. Think about the things you've seen, the things you've experienced, and the views you have about love today. Who taught you how to love? Who taught that person how to love? Is that what you want from love? Do you have someone who loves you the way you need to be loved? Really evaluate this thing we call love. Is what you're calling love *really* love? Be completely honest with yourself. Did you build on the wrong foundation? Did you ignore the red flags? Did you get married out of a sense of obligation? Ask yourself those necessary questions and answer with sincerity.

Love isn't found; it's *created*. Loving can be difficult because it requires you to be selfless. Love must be mutual, because if one person is being selfless and the other is being selfish, love becomes self-hate.

These days, my heart aches for many because of the current state of love. I lived through some tough lessons in love and relationships, so I started teaching what I've learned. From there, thousands of people started reaching out to me for insight. People wanted my help to navigate through the ups and downs of their relationships. It showed me that we are grasping at straws. We are in such a bad place that we will reach out to absolute strangers for help. I've been there myself. As I read through my messages, my heart sinks to my feet over and over again. Some of the revelations I read are just unbelievable. At times I'm brought to tears after reading an email. Other times, I'm angry. In most cases, I'm in shock and disbelief. Relationship struggles do not discriminate. I read emails and messages from well-to-do people. I read emails from people who were raised in stable homes, whether a single-parent home or a two-parent home. I read emails from people who are older than my parents. I read emails from people who are of all different races and socioeconomic backgrounds. I read messages from people located around the world and in many different walks of life. One thing I've realized is that love and pain are universal languages. We all desire love, and we all suffer on the journey. To be honest, I get tired of talking about love and relationships. But I feel it is my duty to share. I know it's my purpose because I have an intricate understanding of it that isn't common. In the past, I didn't know that, but it has become evident over the years, as nearly 3 million people follow me online for the messages I share. As I tour the world speaking on love, I find that we all struggle in the same ways. We are all lost at some point, but not enough people are circling back to help others once they've found their way. I really hurt when I read and hear about the pain that millions of people endure in the name of love. It is a familiar pain I also lived through, and I aim to help others learn how to overcome it and heal from it.

There is a type of man who believes that love means he can control a woman. This is a man who believes that his woman is his property. He believes he can come and go as he pleases and she will always be there waiting. He believes that he can have freedom of choice and freedom of consequence. This man believes he is invincible and his woman will always be a pawn. I find this type of man to be much more common than the opposite.

Then I've come in contact with the woman who believes it's her job to nurture and raise an adult man. She believes that it's a man's place to dominate and control her. She believes that being cheated on or beat on comes with the territory. She is hesitant to leave a toxic relationship because she assumes that all relationships will be that way.

Broken men and broken women reinforce each other's flawed beliefs. When we are broken, we build on a faulty foundation, and then we come crashing down. Everyone around us looks at what we went through and they see the pain but label it as "love." When we tell our version of the story, we say we were in love but it all turned sour. Our testimonial of the relationship also screams that love is pain. Our friends, family members, and children see that play out, and the cycle is continued. That is one of the reasons why divorce rates continue to rise. That is why so many men look like predators and so many women have lost their glow. We don't know love, but we know pain and mistakenly confuse the two.

That all stops now. Welcome to the revolution of real love! It's time to hit the restart button, empty the trash, and fill your life back up with real love. It's time to break the generational curses and start creating generational blessings. Things won't change unless you purposefully make the change. Your change will create a ripple effect, even if only for your family. Your family will require anyone they encounter to elevate to this new level of living. Each one reach one. You will be in a mind-set to help one another and lift one another up. You will have the power to change the world one by one. Love is real. Love is a gift, and it's the greatest gift given to mankind. It's time to walk in love, but first you have to know real love. It will not be easy, but nothing worth doing is effortless. Loving yourself and setting new standards for your life will be difficult, because for once in your life, you will have to put yourself first. It's time to know love!

Ask yourself these questions and write down the answers:

1. Who influenced the way you see love?

2. Did they have the type of love you want?

3. Do you know their pain?

4. Do you know their skeletons?

5. Could what you don't know about them hurt you?

6. Are you willing to set new standards for yourself?

7. Are you willing to do the work it takes to truly love yourself?

8. Are you committed to learning and growing?

9. What is the biggest lie that you've learned about love?

10. What are you going to do to find the truth about love?

Not all of those questions may apply to you, but at least they will get your wheels turning. It's important that you evaluate your teachers of love. It's important that you set your own bar for love and not live beneath someone else's standard. It's important that you remain optimistic about love and the possibilities for your life.

two

DO YOU HATE YOURSELF?

That's a strong question, but it addresses a very common issue that many people struggle with. Throughout our lives, we are bombarded with opportunities to hate ourselves just a little bit more. From grade school all the way up the corporate ladder, there are comparisons and interactions that can influence us to lower our standards. Sometimes it's simply based on what we've learned over the years. There are two sides to this coin. On one side, there are those who hate themselves, so they hurt others. On the other side, you have those who hate themselves, so they allow others to hurt them.

Today I see women who put up with anything and everything. Most likely, this has always been the case, but today it's more blatant. So many women become dependents. The man takes care of the woman financially and sexually, but he starves her emotionally and mentally. Then, because he's taking care of her financially, she bases her entire life on her financial needs being met. She has a roof over her head, food to eat, and clothes to wear, so how much does a happy heart matter? She questions herself. She questions her happiness. She wonders if the dreams of love and happiness she had at a young age were all just fairy tales. Even the bare minimum that she should receive is forgone. She relinquishes her power into the hands of a grown-boy. She forgets her hopes, her dreams, and who she is. Her focus is on chasing him. Her time is spent nurturing him. She's pushing aside her own needs to meet his. All the while, he's depleting her. He's stealing her joy, peace, and happiness. In return he gives her his money and sometimes not even that. He can make more money, but she comes with only one heart. When her heart is broken, mended, and then broken again, she reaches a point of not knowing if she can ever truly love again—not just love a man but also love herself. She feels lost. He never finds himself. All of his toxic behaviors are being reinforced, and he becomes more of who he shouldn't be, while she loses everything that she was meant to be.

Women are nurturers by nature. Men are providers by nature. But when men fail to realize that providing doesn't refer to only finances, women become devoid of real love. The woman becomes a handmaid instead of the queen she was intended to be. The man becomes a slave master, driving her into the ground. Sometimes these roles are flipped around, but neither way is the way of real love.

Where did you lose yourself? When did you forget who you are supposed to be? Who did it to you? What did it to you? Do you love yourself the way you're supposed to? Do you require the people in your life to love you the way you deserve to be loved?

Many women today are nurturing grown-boys. Women today are taking men and making them sons instead of husbands. A woman forgives her son over and over again because he's her son. He came from her, so she feels eternally obligated to protect and provide for him regardless of his mistakes. Her blood runs through his veins, so she's tied to him in a much deeper way. In her mind, his mistakes become her mistakes, so she does everything she can to fix them. She runs behind her son, attempting to steer him in the right direction, and no matter what he does, she never stops loving him. With a son, that could be understood, but with a man who is supposed to be a responsible leader, that cannot be the case. A woman should never have to chase a man who is supposed to meet her halfway. A woman should never have to hurt over and over again because a man refuses to love her the way she deserves to be loved. A woman should not have to raise a grown man. A woman should not have to suffer at the hands of another human. A man should not put a woman through pain that her creator wouldn't put her through.

If you are that woman, you may need to do some soul-searching. Where did you lose your hopes and dreams of the happy marriage and white picket fence? Who hurt you beyond repair? When did you stop trying to love yourself? When did you start to accept less than the best and convince yourself that it was okay? Are you willing to get back up? Are you willing to start over? Are you willing to set new standards for your life, pick up the pieces, and move forward? This is the time to move; it's time that you elevate to the level of living intended for you. Life is too short to settle.

I've seen women stay in relationships after being emotionally, mentally, and physically beaten; fight another woman over a man who cheated; settle for men who refuse to sacrifice their vices for their women; settle for men who refuse to stop cheating; settle for men who repeatedly stepped out on them, impregnating other women; single-handedly try to serve as Narcotics Anonymous for men; allow their hearts to be trampled on; forsake the love and teachings of their parents to chase after grown-boys. What is this madness other than self-hate? It is learned behavior that has become the norm. These are the cases of self-hate that I encounter most often.

As for the men, I have been that man who hated himself. At the time, I would never have admitted that. In my mind, I thought I loved myself. I thought loving myself meant controlling, manipulating, and deceiving the woman in my life. As I grew older and looked back over my life, I realized that self-hate is passed down. We take our own pain, and we pass it down to others. Life is kicking our butt, so we want to make someone pay for our pain and misfortune. We take the pain we've felt and dish it out to someone else. If we have to hurt, someone else has to suffer with us.

As men, we tend to ignore the positive examples of manhood and gravitate toward the negative examples. This negativity provides us an excuse to act out of pain and rage. It's easier to be a victim of the system and then lash out at others. It takes too much strength and courage to be a bigger man, turn the other cheek, and grow from pain and experiences. We take the easy route—or so we think. We can't control ourselves, so we attempt to control someone else. We feel like nothing, so we want to make a woman feel like less than nothing so we can feel like something. We hurt her, lie to her, deceive her, and mislead her. We want to be the leader, but we don't know where we're going. We want to be treated like a king but refuse to treat her like a queen. We want all the power, but we refuse to recognize her influence. We get upset when we are called out on our shortcomings and failures. We want the title as the head, the leader, and the man, but we don't want the responsibility that comes along with it. When it gets too hot in the kitchen, we want to switch places with the woman. We want to shine a light on her flaws instead of our own. We fail to realize the instances when a man caused most of her flaws. When a man steps up to be a positive example for us, we get angry with him for raising the bar of expectation. We're upset because it's so much easier to leave things the way they are, no matter how imbalanced and dysfunctional. It's so much easier to get away with murder if there's no judge and jury. We don't want to be held accountable. Do we really understand what it means to be the head of a household? Do we really want to be leaders? Do we really want to be the best that we can be? Are we all that we claim to be?

This is all so painful. I know it's painful because self-hate causes pain. We cause pain because we've been put through so much pain. Some of us were raised so cold that we have no idea how to be warm. I get it. If that is your personal experience, I understand where you are coming from, but it's not a good enough excuse anymore. It's time that we evaluate the hate from where we operate. Is it hurting only you, or is it hurting someone else?

Have you heard of the "kick the cat syndrome"? In this story, the boss yells at the man while he's at work, the man goes home and yells at his wife, then his wife yells at their son, and then their son kicks the cat. That's how many of us are living today. We don't realize the pain that is being passed down. A broken woman cannot raise happy, healthy children. It's impossible. A broken man cannot lead a happy, healthy household. It's impossible. If you are operating from self-hate, everything around you has the potential to crumble.

To make any relationship work, you have to have a healthy dose of love. You have to face your pain and be willing to make a change. You can't run from the pain; you have to run *through* it. It's so easy to think you've escaped it, but it traps you in other ways. You may have a long relationship, but that doesn't mean you have a happy one. If you compromise your morals and values, you won't have total happiness. You may be in a marriage and have someone to lie next to every night, but that does not equate to happiness if you've forgotten who you are. When you truly love yourself, you realize who you are and what you want out of life. It doesn't matter who you encounter; no one looks better to you than yourself. You may run into your equal, but you will never see yourself as less than anyone else. You will stand your ground in any relationship and demand to be treated the way you treat yourself. You won't lose yourself; you'll see your value. You will know that as long as you have love for yourself, you'll never go wrong in life. So many people have settled for being shells of themselves. They've settled because they don't possess the self-assurance to stand on their own two feet. They feel less than unworthy and incapable of making their own way. They've been dealt a bad hand, and they don't feel like they can fold that hand and start over fresh. Starting over doesn't always mean leaving a relationship. It could mean just sitting down and getting clarity on what's needed in the relationship to make it work. It could mean forgiving each other and starting with a clean slate. On the other hand, it could mean leaving a toxic relationship and making it work with the right person. Both parties have to want to make it work, have to want to be better, and have to be willing to put in the work.

When you love yourself the way you wish someone else loved you, you hold the key to your life. You have to realize that you can be or have anything you want in this world if you love yourself enough. You may have no money and have a rich partner. Your partner may have given you the world in terms of material things. Your partner may have also given you a lot of laughs and good times, but then things changed. Your partner takes his or her time and money and starts to build with someone else. They end up in a full-blown affair with that person, and it re-sults in a pregnancy. Now what do you do? These are situations that get really complicated. It's in those tough times when you really find out who you are. You may decide to give your partner another chance, but under what conditions? Are you going to continue to allow yourself to be lied to, cheated on, and mistreated? Or are you going to lay new ground rules and establish better communication and understanding? If another affair happens years down the road, what will you do? Will you forgive again and stay? Or will you walk away? The key isn't just to make it work. The key is to make it work with the right person. A lot of times when we're dating, we try to make it work with the wrong person, and no matter how hard we try, it just won't work out. You can't make a square peg fit into a round hole.

Identify what it is you dislike about yourself so you can begin the work to reverse those lies. Don't allow life to beat you up and make you feel less than. If you believe you're worth it, you'll receive it. You can't settle. The reason you see people who are not as attractive as you, as smart as you, or as successful as you in happy relationships is that they refused to settle. They knew what they wanted and held to it. There are a lot of good-looking people who feel ugly on the inside. There are a lot of smart people who do dumb things in relationships. There are a lot of successful people in unsuccessful marriages. You don't get what you're worth; you get what you demand. You have to love yourself enough to stand your ground and do what's best for you. Don't give up on your dream for true love. True love does exist. It is very real. I wouldn't be writing this book if I didn't know that to be true. It won't always be con-venient and easy, but it also won't break you down and take advantage of your heart!

Ask yourself these questions:

1. What is the most painful thing you've experienced?

2. What things happened to you that shaped the way you see yourself?

3. Did you get professional help to deal with the pain?

4. Did you change the way you view yourself?

5. Is your relationship's status what you want it to be?

6. Is it getting better?

7. What work will you do to love yourself more and make your relationship situation better?

8. Can you forgive and let go of the past?

9. Are you hurting someone else from your pain?

10. Can you see the pain in those you love?

three

THEY ARE NOT WINNING

If you look around, you'll notice that our society promotes sexual immorality. Consider how the media normalize it. Commercials, movies, articles, and key figures promote promiscuity daily. It's part of the evolution of the world. Our technology has given us so much freedom. Our world is advancing so fast that we start to feel invincible because of all the things we can do with a smartphone. Everything is at our fingertips. Swipe left. You can meet your date for tonight without leaving your house. Just swipe. Then send a cute message. Bam! You're in. It's instant gratification. By making dates so readily available, it increases our fail rate. Before you know it, the list of sexual partners you've scored is becoming reprehensible. It's a free-for-all. There are internet challenges and movements that encourage the behavior. The "shoot your shot" movement urges us to "hit on" persons of interest. There is also "cuffing season," which is around the winter months and refers to getting physically and intimately close to someone during that time. It all sounds like a joke, but in reality there are subconscious impulses being sent and people really do begin to look for someone to cuddle with. Body counts are increasing casually, but there's actually no such thing as casual sex. Those who defy relationship traditions promote sexual freedom. Girlfriends who are playing "wife" tell about their sexcapades. Boyfriends who fear long-term commitment encourage women to have open relationships. I once thought those ideas were reserved for the rich and famous, but while coaching couples around the globe, I have found that everyday people are experimenting with open relationships.

The more you hear about open relationships, the more normal they seem. The couples who are in those relationships appear to be happy, and so the argument for them becomes more convincing. Depending on the type of person you are, a part of you may want an open relationship, too. If you are not that type of person, the thought of it may make you sick to your stomach. I try not to judge but instead just pay close attention. After coaching so many couples in open relationships with threesomes and foursomes, I began to notice patterns. My findings do not stem from a specific couple but from a collection of the most common experiences of many couples.

On the female side, I sensed that the women really wanted to be loved. In most cases, the woman hadn't had a close relationship with her parents or there was a void in her heart from some point in her life. Sometimes the void came from distant or cold parents. Other times, the void came from ex-lovers who had failed to love her the way she deserved. That void left a hole needing to be filled. She hoped that the void would be filled with love. Instead, the void was sensed by someone and then exploited as a weakness. Her ideals of love were turned upside down. Slowly but surely, she lost her truth, and a twisted truth became her own. She initially thought love should be between two people exclusively. Instead, she was told that monogamy is impossible and that it's natural and totally acceptable to sleep with multiple people while in a committed relationship. She was told that the reason why her past relationships didn't work is because they tried to live up to this unnatural, impossible standard of monogamy. It began to make sense to her because, in fact, all of her relationships had failed. She began to think to herself, *Why not try something new?* She opened up to inviting other women into her bed and began to watch her man indulge. She felt pain and confusion, but she grew a thicker skin and made herself pretend to enjoy it until it felt like a norm.

Then something would start to happen. She would start to grow feelings for the woman, or her man would start to grow feelings for the woman. The other woman would start to come around more often. Sneaky sexcapades began to happen. The man's next request was to have sex alone with other women. That didn't sound fair, but the more she thought about it, the more it made sense. She just wanted love. She'd tried it the traditional way and failed time and time again. Why not try this new way? She tried it, and it seemed to be working. Her boyfriend was smiling more. He was happy and loving more often than not. This new open relationship thing seemed to be the answer to the lifelong question of how to make a relationship work.

The longer this carried on, the stronger the ties grew. Sex is spiritual. The very act of sex is to reproduce another being. Two spirits join, creating life from a physical, spiritual, and supernatural manifestation. Isn't that divine? Think about the millions of moving parts interworking to create life. Can you design a human to work like that? Has anyone ever designed a human to operate like that? If you ever have questioned God, reproduction is a strong case for the existence of God. Even when contraceptives are introduced and reproduction is blocked, all the elements that take place to reproduce still happen. Your body goes through all the same motions, emotions, thoughts, and feelings. You may strive to keep it casual and simply ignore the truth of it all. Perhaps you have grown accustomed to sweeping it under the rug. If you continue to sweep it all under the rug, one day the pile will be so big, it may cause you to trip and fall flat on your face.

Sex has a specific purpose. It can't be abused, or it will, in turn, hurt you worse. In open relationships and promiscuous lifestyles, the sex eventually catches up to you. The feelings become too great to be ignored. You'll start to hurt. You'll start longing for more. You want more than just sex. You want a real connection. You want a commitment. Sure, being faithful to one person for life sounds like a tall order, but you want to take the challenge. Your heart isn't designed to be passed around. Eventually you start to feel the tolls you've been paying. Your spirit is weakening. Your soul is aching. You're longing for comfort and peace.

Sex leads to all kinds of feelings. For the female, there is great potential for jealousy to set in. The woman starts to wonder if her man is slowly becoming someone else's man. She starts to wonder if she is becoming the other woman instead of the other way around. She starts to wonder why she's the one being asked to share. Why isn't another man being invited to the bedroom instead of another woman? Why can't she go out and sleep with other men? Deep down, she does not want another man. She wants only her man, but he wants community sex. She starts to realize that this thing is one-sided. She's doing all the sacrificing. She's doing all the compromising. He's not allowing her to entertain other men, nor is he suggesting it. So how is this pleasure for them both? Her senses start to tingle, and the truth is growing more and more obvious. It's becoming very evident that her man wants to have the best of everything, while she settles for pleasing him. Something isn't right here.

In coaching the men in these open relationships, I began to discover many similarities between men and women. A man in this scenario is confused about what real love looks like. Perhaps he was not raised in a home where he saw his father being faithful to his mother. Maybe he views marital bliss as a figment of a woman's imagination. His belief is that in order for a man to be happy in a relationship, he must be free to sleep with multiple women. It's unrealistic to be with one woman for the rest of his life. He has constraints put on him in every aspect of life. He does not want any constraints in his relationship. He has never tried to be completely faithful to a woman, and nothing in him makes him think that he can accomplish such a feat. He feels doomed before even trying, so why try? On the male side of this argument, it's common for the man to say he's never met many faithful men. After seeing his father, brothers, cousins, and friends cheat, he sees no point in trying to be different. It's a man's world, or so he thinks.

Both parties in these losing relationships are victims of an immoral and lost society—a society of division and chaos, not a society of cohesion and forward progress. Just as it seems that the morality of the world around them is collapsing, their relationship is collapsing in the same fashion.

There were a few things I noticed that these couples did not consider. One is the power of lust. In most cases, the open relationship feeds the man's lust. This lust, when fed, becomes not content but insatiable. The man, when giving in to his lustful pleasures, becomes consumed by the flames of his lust. One woman becomes two women. Two women become three women. One escapade leads to another, and the excitement never stops. Lust, unlike thirst, can't be quenched. Once you give in to lust, it requires that you continue to feed it more of the same thing. It will grow and even intensify and may create the desire to try new things, seeking heightened pleasure. This pleasure is fleeting. Ultimately, this lustful pleasure leads to pain, not happiness. Lust is a gateway drug. It may start out small and simple, but it will lead to larger problems, introducing chaos and confusion into any situation. You invite it in, and it takes over. You can't invite the Devil into your bed and then expect him to know his place. So often, I'd coach a woman who allowed her man to entertain other women, and then one of the women entertained on the side would become his new main woman. The cycle repeats itself until the man eventually has an awakening and decides he wants to give traditional love a try. Then the woman who allowed an open relationship loses her man to a closed relationship that shuts her out.

The other thing these couples did not consider are the ties that bind. With every person we lie down with, we take a piece of him or her with us and vice versa. In Corinthians 6:18 (New International Version) it reads, "Flee from sexual immorality. All other sins a person commits are outside of the body, but whoever sins sexually, sins against their own body." Sex cannot be casual because the act is so powerful. You are tying your soul to every person you have sex with, which is why the act has lasting effects on your mind and body. That is why you have visions of that person. That is why after sex or a sexual relationship, you may experience stomachaches, sleepless nights, loss of appetite, dreams, nightmares, and so on. Sometimes you could be sitting or lying down, and it's almost like you can feel the person's body. Sex is not only physical, it is spiritual. It is one of the most powerful human connections known to mankind. Sex can bring us closer than blood relations. People turn their backs on friends and family for sexual partners. People ignore all rational thinking and common sense for sex. Sex confuses. Sex binds. Sex entraps. Sex can be everything it's not supposed to be if it is used out of context. This can cause a great deal of pain. Even the attachments you did not bargain for become tied to you. When you lie down with someone, you're not only lying with that person, you are lying with everyone else he or she has ever known sexually.

After observing couples closely, I noticed they began to take on each other's ways. Sex joined them so closely that they began to share attitudes, mind-sets, and beliefs. The wiser of the two can brainwash the other to believe anything he or she wishes. Someone gets lost in the sin of sex. Confusion sets in, and happiness is no more.

I share all of this to refute the idea that those who don't practice monogamy are winning. It looks good online and in the movies, but behind closed doors, the dream is a nightmare. Many women today are growing frustrated because they assume that women who are promiscuous are more successful in relationships. Promiscuous women may, in fact, have more relationships and spend less time single, but that does not equate to happiness. A woman in an open relationship or a woman who has casual sex wants to be loved just like any other woman. What she keeps discovering is that the men she's entertaining do not want to love her back. She's learning that she wants a man to herself, and when she tries to give him what he wants and allow him to have multiple women, it backfires. She's learning that his desire for multiple women isn't manhood, it's boyhood. She's learning that she's lost, confused, and hurting. She's learning that she's trying to fill her voids by lowering her standards, but being desperate won't fix her. She cries most nights. She wears a self-assured face for the public, but on the inside she's dying. She's in love with a lost, confused man who is only trying to find his way. He's not a grown man. He's a grown-boy. She wants better. She wants more. Her fear is that if she sets higher standards, she'll be single like you. She admires your strength, but she isn't there yet. She's hoping you will keep the faith and keep the strength, because you are her inspiration. While you're envying her, she's admiring you. She wishes she had the confidence, strength, and security to remain single until the right man comes along and dedicates himself to her only. But the pain she's suffered has her screaming out for attention and companionship. She can't stand to be alone because the darkness is too dark and the silence is too quiet. She would rather have half a man than no man. To her, pain is better than no feeling at all. She has substituted companionship for happiness, regardless of how bad it hurts. She knows it won't work, but she keeps taking her chances, hoping that one day she will be enough of a woman for a man to fully commit. Pray for her, don't envy her.

The man she attracts and keeps is not ready to be a whole man. He feels lost. He feels confused. He is intelligent enough to know that settling down with one woman is the right thing to do, but he lacks the strength and fortitude to do it. He keeps telling himself that one day he may be able to commit to one woman, but as long as he can find a pretty woman to accept him and his flaws, he won't change. He's fighting everything that he knows is right. He actually doesn't want a woman who is whole and has a pretty clean past. The dirtier a woman's past, the better she is for him. He recognizes that she has a lot of life experiences that have hurt her. She's primed for more abuse. Oh, just a little mental abuse first, then a dash of verbal abuse, and every now and then a little physical abuse. Then rinse it off with a shopping spree, flowers, a nice card, and a few weeks of the dream relationship. Then, after the rinse, repeat. He loves the type of woman whom society labels a "hoe." He knows she has just the right amount of brokenness to be manipulated. He knows he can convince her that it's what she wants. She will tell herself that she wants other women in their bed just like he does. She will tell herself that she understands that men cheat, and she would never expect a man to be faithful to only her. She will say that men who claim to be 100 percent faithful are liars and she'd rather be with a man who at least is honest about his needs. He reinforces all of the beliefs. He gets her to believe that it's her wish just as much as his. He can sleep at night because he doesn't feel like he's forcing her to do anything; this is what she wants after all. They find a way to function in dysfunction, until they can't. The relationship ends after a long run.

Ironically, these types of broken relationships outlast a lot of traditional relationships. The pain and confusion become addicting. The up-and-down roller-coaster ride makes for an exciting time. Who wants to be bored in love? At least that's what they tell themselves. When it ends, it's simply chalked up as a fun time. They walk away and claim there is no hate or animosity toward the other party. Typically, within a month and sometimes within a week, these individuals are in another "situationship." A lot of times, it's with someone who was connected to or a part of the broken relationship. That person was waiting for it to fall apart so he or she could take someone's spot. That's the cycle I've seen play out over and over again.

So when you see someone who seems to be taking shortcuts to love, having sex on the first night, getting engaged within a few months, sleeping with multiple people, posting their naked body online, and always in a relationship, it's not always what it seems. Keep your standards. It's okay to desire a relationship that is 100 percent faithful and committed. It's okay to be stingy about sex and to save yourself for marriage. In fact, that's what the Bible says. It's okay to dress and behave in a conservative manner for the public and save the naughty side for your spouse. All of that is perfectly okay. Don't feel the need to do what you see others doing. Don't compare yourself with others. It may take you longer to achieve your goals, but when you reach them, you may experience more lasting results.

Here are some things to think about:

1. Have you ever envied the promiscuous people you know? If so, why?

2. Have you ever been a promiscuous person? If so, why?

3. Break your soul ties! Cut off your exes. Detox from them on social media, phone, and elsewhere. Get a new knowledge of love and relationships, and continue your healing process.

4. Do you understand why sex should not be casual, or do you disagree?

5. Have you ever seen a promiscuous person really win in love?

6. Know this: If you take shortcuts, you will get cut short!

7. Keep your eyes on your journey and stop comparing yourself to others.

8. Don't envy. Pray!

9. Do it God's way because your way will fail.

10. The goal is to be whole!

four

BELIEVE WHAT THEY CONSISTENTLY SHOW YOU

One of the dilemmas I read about the most relates to women who have been in a relationship for nearly a decade or more and the man still hasn't changed. Each year, this woman has held out hope that something would miraculously change him, but each year, she has been let down. Now, after several years, she's at the end of her rope. She's lost, confused, and hurting and needs some advice about what she should do from here. After reading these stories, I always feel a sense of hopelessness. There is so much pain that has been caused. There are so many unpardonable offenses. The pain, hate, and resentment run deep. It's not even a relationship anymore. It seems like an emotional torture experiment being run by some prestigious university. It makes me count my blessings, but it also makes me hurt to know that so many people are suffering through this type of existence and calling it love.

To be honest, in most cases, if it's still toxic after nearly a decade, it's pretty hard to turn it around. It's dangerous to hand out possible fixes at that point in the relationship. It also seems unfair to say, "Just leave." That's obviously not the easiest thing to do, nor do many people want to hear that. Most people cannot fathom wasting a decade of their lives and then just walking away and starting all over. It almost seems easier to just settle and keep living a life that is half miserable and half peaceful. Even though there may be only one day a week of peace, it seems better than to walk away and running the risk of living through the same struggle all over again with the next person.

I wish human beings would focus on the ounce of prevention more than the pound of cure, but rarely do we do that. If you look all the way back to the first date, you may be able to see some things you missed at the time. First, you have to recognize what was shown to you. Then you have to recognize the things the other person *consistently* shows you. A person can't help but be who he or she is. *A person playing a role will eventually forget their act.* Everything a person does is telling you something about them. Pay attention to their personality traits and habits. Take each thing you notice and multiply it by three. With time and complacency, all of their adverse behaviors are likely to be multiplied by three. That's a happy-medium figure with which to assess your tolerance of that behavior.

Let's look at some common behavior traits, personality traits, and habits.

Arguing or Debating. When talking to a person you've just met and are considering dating, pay attention to how often they oppose your thoughts. It's great to have someone who speaks his or her mind. How do they voice their opinions? Are the opinions based in reality? Can you see their points? Can you respect their points? How often do they feel the need to oppose what you're saying? Is this your personality, too? Do you like debating? Do you like arguing your points? Now imagine you're five years into the relationship and super comfortable with each other. Multiply the debates by three. Can you handle it? Can you keep it up for another forty years?

Lying. It's common for people to tell small lies in the beginning of a relationship. Some of the lies seem insignificant. He may say he earns $60,000 but really he earns $50,000, and if he gets bonuses and commissions, he will hit $60,000, but he's never actually done it. She may say she never talks to her ex and she's over him, but really they speak once a week. He may say he was at the gym working out, but really he was at his friend's house playing video games. She may say she was at Starbucks working on a proposal, but really she was at the gym working out with her female friend. The little lies may seem insignificant, but a lie is a lie. Little lies eventually become big lies. You catch the other person in a lie, but you ignore it because it seems so pointless. You're baffled at why someone would even think to lie about something so simple. A lie is hiding something. A lie is a clue to something much deeper. Fast-forward ten years. The relationship is growing stale. The thrill is gone. Now the lies come three times as often and are three times as serious. What would a lie that size be about? Can you handle it? Can you build a relationship on lies? Can lies sustain a relationship? If he or she cheated on you, how hard would it be for him or her to tell one more lie after all the lies they've already told?

Insecurity. In the beginning, insecurity is almost always cute because of the way it shows up. He makes a weight joke because she finished her food faster than he did. She makes a pouty face, gets up, and walks away. He laughs it off. She has a little attitude, but it blows over after five minutes. They carry on. She's on the phone with her dad, laughing and shooting the breeze. He tells her in a playful serious manner that she can't talk to any other men in front of him and that he needs to be the only man in her life. She laughs about it. He says he's serious with a humorous facial expression. They carry on. Fast-forward ten years. She's gained thirty pounds. She's insecure about her weight, so she doesn't want to be cuddly or intimate. It pushes him away. The insecurity that was innocent is now fully grown and breaking down the relationship. At around the same time in the relationship, she's the team mom of her son's football team. She's talking to the coach about the next practice. After she's done, her man looks at her with a rude look. She asks him what's wrong. His insecurity makes him give her the silent treatment for the next hour. She realizes it's because he's implying that she is attracted to her son's football coach. The insecurity that was cute in the first month is now scary and sad.

Excessive Cursing and Name Calling. He loves to tell jokes and always interjects curse words to make it funnier. She loves to curse to sound like the cool chick. They have a good time using the street slang and internet meme curse phrases of the month. Fast-forward five years. They are extremely familiar and comfortable with one another now. They're arguing, and he calls her a b**ch. She hurls a few choice words of her own in his direction. They both take the words to heart. The words become weapons, and they wound. The wounds don't heal, because before they get a chance to, another violent argument breaks out and reopens the very wounds they were trying to heal. The cursing and the name-calling aren't so cute now.

Drinking and Using Recreational Drugs. It's fun. It's cool. It's normal. Everyone gets drunk on the weekends. Everyone smokes weed, or so they say. Fast-forward ten years. What was recreational is now necessary. When the alcohol or weed isn't in the system, the boat rocks. People are moody, on edge, feisty, and fed up. They said it was just for fun and a pastime, not actually a habit. They said they didn't need it and could quit at any time. Now it is a necessity. Now the baby is inhaling smoke or lying on the skin of marijuana-filled pores. Oh, the beer bottle was left on the coffee table with just a few sips left in it. The toddler got ahold of it and drank it. A little weed in the pores and alcohol in the system never hurt a baby, right? The recreational fun is suddenly a serious problem. You're asking the other person to stop smoking or drinking, but your partner doesn't see the problem. You want to raise a happy, healthy, functional family, but the substances seem to have too much control. You missed the signs.

The Crushable Friends. He had a lot of female friends who used to like him or vice versa. She had a lot of male friends who once made a pass or two at her. It's all part of fun conversation. Everyone knows everyone. Everyone is cool. Fast-forward ten years, and the inappropriate gestures and conversations that you let fly a while back have resurfaced. Due to complacency, your relationship is struggling. The "crushable friend" has been waiting in the wings, still single, and always ready to console. Now the friendship seems to be something more. It's crossing the line, and the confidentiality they are keeping is making you uncomfortable. You ask that it be cut off, but at this point it seems the crushable friend has more value than you do.

The Third-Wheel Parent. She talks to her mom four times a day. He talks to his mom four times a day. All is cool. It's cute that he's so close to his mom. It's cute that she and her mom have that close sisterhood. Fast-forward five years. You're in the middle of an argument, and Mom is knocking on the door. You have to stop the conversation because Mom has popped up unannounced. This happens over and over again. You're out on a date, and the phone keeps lighting up. You have to check the phone just in case the sitter is calling about the kids. It's Mom. She keeps calling to check in because she hasn't had her fourth conversation of the day yet. She won't stop calling until she has the fourth call. Oh, he forgot to inform his mom that tonight is date night, so he needs to interrupt the date to inform Mom so she can rest easy. In another incident, they are having a discussion and she keeps mentioning how her dad took so much better care of her than he is doing. Ten years ago, he thought it was amazing to know she had her father in her life. Now he can't seem to ever be good enough because his wife is still married to her father in her mind. The overbearing parent was cute for the first three months of dating. Ten years in, and now you're on the verge of divorce because of it.

Bromance and Girls' Night. He's always playing video games or hanging with the boys. His work has him around men all the time, so it makes sense for him to be close with them. She loves to kick back and have a couple drinks with the girls. They share the gossip of the week and recap all their favorite shows. Fast-forward ten years. He's at the club with his single friend who just went through a bad breakup. She's on the phone with her friend, telling every detail about every argument they've had for the last month. He talks to his boys more than he talks to her. She confides in her girl before confiding in her man. They get more satisfaction from their friends than they do from each other. It was great to have friends in the beginning, but they never found balance. Now it seems like they'd be better off dating their friends than being in a relationship with each other.

———————

Those are just some of the issues people bring to me. There are always red flags when dating, but you may have chosen to ignore them. Some things need to be ignored, while other things need to be addressed. Since you were a child, you may have heard the saying "too much of anything isn't good for you." Love is a moral act, so you have to evaluate your partner's morals and actions. If the morals are low, the love will be bad. If the actions are poor, the love will be lacking. You have to pay attention to the signs and use them to determine how to move forward.

Address the issues you feel need to be tackled. Be open-minded when addressing your concerns. Listen to your partner's reasoning around that issue. Then continue to observe and examine behavioral patterns. After a decade of marriage, I notice that the same flaws my wife and I had in the beginning are still with us. We can live with our flaws. Our flaws are not deal breakers. The problem with a lot of relationships is that the flaws are excuses to call it quits. If one of my flaws was cheating, I wouldn't still be married today. My wife spends money differently than I do. I just had to learn how to adjust to the amount of money she may want to spend on our son's birthday parties and family get-togethers. If she needed the attention of other men, we wouldn't still be married today. Some perceived imperfections a person shows you are actually just differences that can be manageable. You have to know the difference between a fault that can be managed and a weakness that can shut down the entire operation. Is it a core issue or not?

You have to pay attention to what you are being shown. If the behavior is detrimental and it shows up over and over again, take heed. I jokingly mentioned that my wife spends too much. She does spend, but no more than any other woman in her position. If she were hocking my stuff online to feed a shopping addiction, we would have a problem.

When you address an issue, you have to resolve it. If there is an aggressive streak in your partner, you have to address it at the verbally aggressive stage. You have to call him or her out on it and let it be known from the get-go that it will not be tolerated. Don't wait until the fifth time it happens to address it. By then it's a habit. If there are lies, you have to call your partner out on the lies immediately. Let him or her know right away that you're hip to the game and the lies won't fly. If there are addictions or habits that seem to be innocent but you can tell they can easily get out of hand, confront the other person. If you don't want a partner who smokes, tackle it. If it's something he or she can't rectify or let go, that should not influence you to settle. It simply means that that person is not for you. If you don't want to curse in your communication because you have the foresight to see how it can become violent, say that. If your partner can't see the logic behind your communication rules, he or she is not on the same level as you and will only hold you back from peace and prosperity. Whomever you choose to be with should want to be their absolute best. If who they want to be isn't the type of person you want to be with, keep it moving. There is nothing wrong with making it work, but it is not sensible to force something that's not meant to be. There's a difference between *making* it work and *forcing* it to work. Even when everything lines up perfectly in a relationship, eventually things will get off track and need to be fixed. Nothing will be smooth forever or at all times. Then there are situations where certain pieces just don't fit together. If you force the union, it will be ruined. You can't put Bentley parts into a Volkswagen. It just won't work.

If it is meant to be, changes will be made after the issues have been addressed. As a human being, you have the ability to transform for the better. You just need to know what is expected of you in order to steer your efforts in the right direction. You can be faithful. You can be honest. You can be loyal. You can be trustworthy. You can be an amazing lover. You just need to know the standard of excellence that is required of you in love. Once you know what is required, you are capable of achieving that level of living if you truly desire to reach it. In relationships, the reason some people never change is because they don't care enough to change for you, nor do they care enough to change for themselves. It has been said that a person has to change for him- or herself. In most cases, people change because they are inspired to change by someone else. A man can remain a cheater, but when he makes the decision to be faithful, it is usually because he has met the woman who he feels deserves all of him.

I'm a believer in change because I changed drastically. People who knew me before my marriage don't recognize the man I became in marriage. I am a completely different person. The desire to change was inspired by my wife's demand to be loved on the level she deserves. Yes, I desired change, but I changed for more than just myself. My wife was the ultimate inspiration. Change is possible. Change can happen. We are human, which means we are capable of anything we set our minds to. We built this world we live in using only a portion of our brain capacity. We do not fully understand ourselves or the infinite power and wisdom granted to us by God. So to say a cheater can't change, an abuser can't change, or a liar can't change is to say that God is a lie. God grants man the power to change. I proved the power of change to myself, so I believe the power of change resides in anyone who leans not to his or her own strength.

On the contrary, if a person refuses to change, there is nothing you can do about it. Prayer will not change a person who is unwilling to change. Sticking around will not change a person who is unwilling to change. Having children will not change a person who is unwilling to change. Nothing can stop a person from remaining the same or from changing if that's what he or she desires. As a man thinketh, so he is. Let anyone who refuses to change remain the same. Unless you plan to change for the worse to be with him or her, step aside and let God work on those who refuse to elevate their lives through self-improvement. If you do not require anything different from this person, do not look up in surprise in ten years if the person is still the same. It will not take a scholar or philosopher to understand the simple fact that he or she remained the same because you remained with him or her. Any behaviors that are recognized and reinforced will continue to be repeated.

Here are some things to think about:

1. Are you ignoring the signs because you're tired of waiting on real love?

2. Do you feel you deserve better than you've been given?

3. Do you fear not being able to find someone who meets your standards?

4. Do you settle out of fear?

5. Know this: If you meet your own standards, you will attract someone who meets them, too.

6. Know this: A person will never change for the better if they believe you'll keep accepting what they've been giving you.

7. Know this: To make love last forever, you must have standards that promote longevity in love.

five

MARRIAGE IS NECESSARY

In the last five years, I've heard people say marriage isn't necessary more than I ever had before. Maybe it was fifty years ago when it wasn't a question whether marriage was necessary or not. I'm sure those who are against marriage have some pretty understandable reasons to view it as a nonessential. One of the reasons is that the divorce rate in America is 50 percent. Why would anyone want to do something that has a 50 percent fail rate? There's also a lot of pressure around weddings. Average people pay for $50,000 weddings, which is $45,000 over their budget. Newlyweds enter marriages upside down in debt and somehow are still expected to stand the test of time. I get it. From a logical standpoint, I understand why so many people are starting families before getting married. Nonetheless, it is alarming to see.

Many people believe marriage is only a Christian thing, but that's not true. Marriage was happening around the world prior to the birth of Christ. In many places around the world, marriage is arranged or forced.

In those cases, it has nothing to do with love. Love is secondary or an afterthought. In some American families, marriages are arranged as well, but it's not something most people would admit. Historically, the goal of marriage was to ensure that a family lineage would continue to thrive. If at some point a generation just decided that marriage and family is no longer the goal, the concern was for the end of mankind. Therefore the institution of marriage was definitely intended for much more than love. Much of the traditional reasoning behind marriage makes sense, but I'm analyzing it in a different light.

To be honest, I cannot recall a woman telling me in a one-on-one conversation that she never wants to be married. There may be many women who do not want to get married, but of the 2.7 million women who support me online, I have never met one. Of the thousands of women I've spoken to personally in coaching sessions and at events around the world, I have never met one. I have met women who are in a season of their lives when marriage is not the goal, but they foresee that the season will change. I have also met women who claim to be on the fence about whether marriage is necessary. I've noticed in those cases that it's largely because they are with men who have been telling them for years that marriage is just a piece of paper and means absolutely nothing. In my opinion, that's a lie. Marriage means a lot, a *whole* lot.

Why would a man tell a woman marriage isn't necessary? The answer is simple: he does not want accountability. If I wanted to swindle you out of money for a service, I would convince you to give it to me without a contract of any sort. I could then steal your money and you would never hear from me again. If we have a contract, you can take me to court and win a judgment against me. I have to honor that judgment or pay the consequences of disobeying it. In most cases, that is why some men say marriage isn't necessary. A man who says marriage isn't necessary wants to be able to cheat on a woman without feeling like he's breaking any laws. He wants to be able to leave her at any given time and not have to split fifty-fifty with her. He wants to be able to take her innocence, her loving, and everything else he can get and not have to worry about the responsibility of a lifetime commitment. In marriage, everything is fifty-fifty, so if a man is the breadwinner and he leaves, he has to lose some of his net worth to do so. That fact coined the phrase "It's cheaper to keep her."

Marriage is necessary because it says, "I'm willing to make a lifelong commitment to another person." It says, "I'm willing to sign on the dotted line, cross my heart, and hope to die if I'm lying." It says, "Just as I wouldn't expect you to do a business deal without a contract, I don't expect you to trust me with your heart without a lifetime commitment." Yes, we can say that with our mouths and mean it, but our world operates on written agreements. If you need a written agreement for monetary transactions, how much more so for matters of the heart? Not everyone sees it like that. Many people trivialize marriage and make the argument that it's only a piece of paper that holds no value. Many say that it's a trap. Many say that it's a curse. All of those reasons are just excuses in my opinion. Those who do not plan to love one person for a lifetime fear marriage. I think marriage is unnecessary if you plan to leave without repercussions. Marriage sets boundaries. Marriage sets expectations. Marriage has rules, regulations, and repercussions if you break the rules. The beauty of marriage is that it makes your intentions known. The intention is to make it last a lifetime. That may not happen, but when you enter a marital space, you are starting with the right intentions. If you claim you don't want marriage but you want someone to give you his or her heart, it sounds like you intend to break it. Why ask for a person's heart but not give that person the assurance in return that you plan to love him or her until death do you part? If your word is your bond and you are a person of your word, then get married. It's hard for us to have complete faith in God. What makes you think we can have complete faith in human words?

Think about this: fifty percent of the marriages in America fail. Imagine the percentage of successful relationships *without* marriage. In my entire lifetime and in all of my experiences, studies, and coaching countless people around the world, I saw one couple last until death did them part without marriage, and the man died before he reached sixty years old. In most cases, you fail in relationships. So the fact that 50 to 60 percent of marriages succeed shows there is something right about marriage. The 50 to 60 percent of marriages succeed because most people mean business when they sign an agreement and recite a vow. We as humans are conditioned to take vows, swears, and written agreements very seriously. The 40 to 50 percent who fail at marriage usually fail because 90 percent of those couples built their union on the wrong foundation.

What I've found is that marriage isn't broken. The people in the marriage are broken. Prior to entering marriage, we don't learn how to make it work. Sometimes, where we're from and who raised us determine our mind-set around marriage. We don't know what percentage of failed marriages include someone who was raised in a single-parent home. Even if the single-parent home was a stable environment for a person in a failed marriage, it still showed them he or she could stand alone. Such people may be less motivated to make the marriage work if they watched their mother do it effortlessly on her own. We don't know what percentage of failed marriages included a person who was rushed, forced, manipulated, or coerced into the marriage. There are many factors that affect the failing rates of marriages today. After being a relationship coach for more than a decade, I was able to see how many relationships we go through trying to find the right person. I realized that 100 percent of our relationships fail until we find the marriage that lasts and changes our personal statistics. I would much rather have a 50 percent chance at succeeding in marriage than a .001 percent chance at succeeding in a situationship. I have watched countless couples do everything married couples do except get married. That piece of paper made a huge difference in the trajectory of their relationship. Without marriage, there is no real commitment. At any time, someone can decide to walk away. There are no lawyers involved. There's no public humiliation or shame that will make them think twice before leaving. They can just wake up one morning and decide they're tired of the situationship and want something new. I have seen relationships with no hope of marriage end after the people in them wasted more than a decade. If they had been married, at least there would have been something to fight for. They would have seriously thought about giving it a real effort before paying lawyers and splitting their assets. Instead, they just said goodbye and walked away. That left someone with a huge hole in his or her heart. A hole that big is very hard to fill. If they had been in a marriage instead of a situationship, they would have had assets to split and could have both walked away with something. Without marriage, sometimes a person is left with nothing and can do nothing about it. In business, the benefit of a contract is the protection it brings. The same applies to marriage. Marriage is a covenant, a covering, and a blessing with protection. Even if it is not successful, there is a written agreement to protect both parties. When you disregard marriage, how do you protect yourself?

I have coached countless women who allowed a man to tell them that marriage isn't necessary. The women proceeded to give the men their life, heart, and love. The men used them, drained them, and, after a decade, left them high and dry. Many of those women lost ten years of life running behind a successful man. Many of the women gave back all the jewelry and gifts because when the man took her desire to marry, he also took her self-worth and self-respect. When she traded in her standards for a moment of convenience, it cost her more than she could imagine. After all those years, many women look back and say "Wow, I should have left after year two or three, when I realized he was never going to marry me." Marriage is not a guarantee that your relationship will succeed, but it's an indicator that the person you love is serious about making it work and has the right intentions.

As a Christian man, I wanted to be married to be pleasing in the eyes of God. According to the Bible, fornication is a sin. That biblical principle carries so much weight because so much comes along with sex. I'd made the mistakes over and over. I'd felt the soul ties without a covenant. If I'm going to be tied to someone spiritually and emotionally, I want a lifetime commitment. The Bible says in Proverbs 18:22: "He who finds a wife finds a good thing, and obtains favor from the Lord."

I came to realize there is no favor from God while having sex outside of marriage. Let this book you're reading be a testament to the favor on my life. I wanted to be in right standing with God. I'd done it my way, and it had always ended in pain, hate, and resentment. I wanted something new. I let Christ and His teachings renew my mind and make me new. Then I did it God's way, and everything in love began to change for the better. So if a man tells me he doesn't believe marriage is necessary, it just lets me know we don't believe in the same God. That's his choice, and I have to respect that. I made my choice, and God showed me that His words would not return void. I stepped into favor. That's my story and I'm sticking to it.

A healthy marriage provides immeasurable benefits. With marriage being a commitment, it brings security. That security allows me to rest. I'm leaning on the covenant to hold the human I married in check. I'm hoping the humanity in her will convict her if she ever thinks about stepping outside of her vows. I'm hoping that her natural inclination to honor her agreements will hold firm. It gives me rest, peace, and security knowing that I am bound to someone who has vowed to love me until death parts us. With that security, there is no need to fear giving my all; we are in this thing forever. I can drop my guard. She can let her hair down. We don't need to front or pretend. When two people are fully committed to each other, there is peace in the midst of tough times. Marriage is so beautiful because in it sex is a blessing rather than a curse. You're blessed for the pleasure you experience in your bedroom because your bed is not defiled. You aren't sharing your body with anyone else, so the two of you belong to each other. God honors that, and He pours out blessings over your union. Your love grows stronger if you keep the main things in focus. If you remember that you're in this together and for life, you're able to make it better because you know it has to last you a lifetime.

In marriage, you are everything to each other. You are best friends. You are lovers. You are doctors and nurses. You are chefs and butlers. You are exotic dancers and teases. You are life coaches and counselors.

You are there through thick and thin. The only requirements are loyalty, honesty, and trust. You can be whole with each other. The world is yours, and everything else comes after you two. I see men flourish in healthy marriages. My studies show me that happily married men earn more money on average and also live longer lives than single playboys do. I see what healthy marriage does for my male clients, and it's mind-boggling to see the difference in peace and clarity between happily married men and single playboys. The success is different with happily married men. The success is more than money; it's fulfillment. Even when there isn't a lot of money, there's a sense of security knowing that eventually the money will be coming. For happily married women, I notice a new confidence. It's a confidence in her mind and body that is different from that of single women fighting against marriage. After coaching countless women, I've noticed that happily married women have more peace than promiscuous women who are trying to beat men at their game. There's an emotional stability that comes with marriage that can't be duplicated anywhere else. Don't think of it as strange when healthy love feels as if it has completed you.

The stability of a healthy marriage is a safe haven for children. Young children are able to see their father treating their mother like a queen. They get to see him sacrifice for the family, and they see her strength as the backbone of the family. They see love come to life, and it sets a precedent of love, safety, and peace. It provides the children with the definition of a home. Success and money may be nice, but nothing beats love. Kids can rest easy. They can spend their days living, laughing, and loving. They do not have to stress and worry; they can rest assured that Mommy and Daddy will make everything all right. This isn't to suggest that the same can't happen in a single-parent home, but if it can happen in a single-parent home, imagine the benefit of a home with a loving marriage of two parents.

A healthy marriage also affects our world. That loving home makes it easier for two loving people to go into society and be productive. These people can give to the world instead of just taking. The children they raise can take this model, go out, and also become productive citizens and add value to the workplace. The world spins a little smoother when resting on the cylinders of real love.

Marriage is very necessary. It is also still very alive and the goal of millions of people. Don't let anyone tell you that your goal of marriage is unrealistic or outdated. There are many benefits to marriage, and the world needs more happy, healthy marriages giving back to the world. It is for the good of our world that we function at our best because we have someone to love and they love us in return. Everything affects everything else, and from the head the blessings flow through the body. Our families affect our society more than anything else. If we are broken in our homes, we will be broken in our world. If we are lacking love in our homes, we will lack love in the world. We must learn how to take care of home before we can take care of anything else. Our world's success will happen from the inside out. Imagine having leaders who were raised by two loving parents who showed them how to be responsible, respectful, reliable, and loving. Think about what it takes to be a criminal. What does it take to steal? What does it take to kill? What does it take to hurt others? Picture those people who have done the unspeakable. Picture the criminals and menaces to society. Now give them a strong father who set a positive example in the home and a loving mother who was equally as strong, nurturing, loving, and caring. Now tell me what love can't cure. Tell me what a strong unit of parents raising children in this world can't accomplish. Sure, there will be some who begin on the strongest foundation and still go astray, but the odds are in our favor with the more love we have in our world.

My goal is to do all I can to bring real love to the forefront in the world and to make healthy marriage the goal of relationships. I see the effect it's having on family and friends, and I've seen what it has done for countless others around me. I believe if we can make this the norm, we can change the world for the better. It will take each of us doing our part.

Here are some things to think about:

1. 50 to 60 percent of marriages succeed.

2. Marriage is for your protection.

3. Until death does us part does not mean until the other person kills you.

4. Just because a marriage fails does not mean you shouldn't try again.

5. What are your honest views around marriage?

6. Have you identified the underlying reasons about why you do or don't want to be married?

7. Is there something that has happened in your life that affected the way you view marriage?

8. If you fail at marriage, will you try again?

9. Do you believe marriage is necessary for those who aren't religious?

10. If you meet the love of your life but have different views on marriage, what will you do?

six

BE SELFLESS

Most marriages fail because people live with a "What have you done for me lately?" mentality. Many go into a relationship looking for what they can get from a person. How much money does my spouse have? How many business connections does my spouse have? How much money will my spouse inherit when his or her parents die? How well can my spouse please me mentally, emotionally, and physically? How much can I get my spouse to do for me? How many gifts will I get on holidays? How many carats will my ring be? How elaborate will my wedding be? How expensive will my house and cars be? Those are the questions people ask when going into a marriage. If taking is the goal, then giving can't be of any importance.

We live in a very selfish, self-centered society. We are conditioned now more than ever to be selfish. How many likes can I get on a post? How many followers can I get online? How many compliments can I get for my outfit of the day? How can I make my haters jealous of my lifestyle? How can I make my relationship look amazing online to make my exes jealous? Many of us live our lives to impress everyone but our spouse. Social media has created monsters in human form. There is so much attention-seeking behavior online that nothing seems to be real anymore. We don't know what to believe and what to overlook. In fact, we begin to believe everything we see online. Jealousy can set in very quickly, so we start to want our own shine.

In a world of superfast technology, we have become even more of a microwave society. Instant gratification is what we seek. We want it now or not at all. We want it hot and fast. It's the "drive-through" society. Microwave love and drive-through service on demand. We want every store app to collect points and get the next purchase free. We take the same mentality into our relationships. We want our spouse to keep track of every good deed we do. Our deeds have motives. We don't do them just to do them. We do them for instant gratification. We do them so we can bring up later how amazing we are. Everything comes with fine print now. The great offer is in big letters, but if you read the small print, it's a trap. Now the traps are being set in our marriages. What can I trick you into this week? He rubs her back for five minutes a night for two nights in a row and then asks for a thirty-minute full-body massage in return. She cooks for him two nights in a row and then asks for a $200 date night on the weekend. If he speaks to her nicely all week, he gets a guys' night out with the boys. If she cooks all week, she gets to go rack up debt on the credit cards at the mall on the weekend.

Relationships fail when the butterflies go away. The butterflies are always fluttering when the relationship is new. After a while, you get to know a person and you're no longer excited about his or her conversations and what he or she has to say. You're just being you and he or she is just being who he or she is. Nothing is new, and nothing is exciting. That is why relationships fail, because we stop working. We get complacent.

I've coached many couples who have gotten complacent. As I listen to each person speak, all I hear is what he or she does for the other person. Neither person takes the time to acknowledge what his or her spouse does for him or her. It's all me, me, me. It's almost like such people are blind to their spouse's efforts because they are so busy keeping count of their own good deeds so they can brag about them later. The man is the best husband in the city, if you let him tell it. The woman is the rarest find of a wife, if you let her tell it. According to their stories about themselves, they each are an amazing catch, but somehow their relationship is a wreck. He does everything under the sun and so does she, yet it sounds like nothing is getting accomplished. They each can see their own worth but not their spouse's worth. He makes the most money, gets up in the middle of the night with the baby, takes out the trash, fixes everything around the house, and is faithful. She cooks, cleans, works a full-time job, takes care of the baby when she can, and even tries to be intimate from time to time. Somehow they can't see their shortcomings, nor do they truly appreciate the other person's efforts. It's all because we are selfish.

Many times, relationships begin with two people who got their way all their life. The man is accustomed to getting his way with women. The woman is accustomed to getting her way with men. Both parties are master manipulators. Both know how to play the victim in the right way at the right time. Both know how to toot their own horn and pat their own back in such a way that it makes their spouse believe they're the best thing since sliced bread or God's gift to mankind. It has worked countless times before, so why shouldn't it work just one more time?

It becomes a real struggle because each is trying to convince the other what a great catch he or she is. They'll even hire a relationship coach or take free counseling at the church to try to convince the other of their worth in the relationship. It's all a power struggle. It's a battle for superiority. Both people in this type of relationship want to be admired, praised, or worshipped. They want to be appreciated to the point where their spouse is constantly seeking their approval. We are so selfish as humans that we will literally let someone serve us every day, and we will accept it as if we deserve it. Then, if we get tired of receiving so much, we will momentarily reciprocate before getting back on our throne. I've seen it happen over and over again. In most relationships, there is a king or queen and his or her servant. There should be mutual respect and mutual benefits in a relationship, but that is not as common as selfishness.

My wife and I went through this very struggle. It all shifted when I decided to lead with love and to be selfless in my ways. I believe selflessness should begin with the man. Men are more prone to getting complacent when on the receiving end. Men have been kings and presidents from the beginning of time. There is something in the male psyche that makes us feel entitled to royal treatment. If a woman is selfless before a man, there is a good chance the man will put his foot on her head and keep her there. If it's the other way around, there's a good chance the woman will feel an urge to reciprocate the love she's receiving. This is on average, but of course there are exceptions.

The reason men should lead with love is that they have been given the upper hand in the world and everything around us has been put in our lives to serve us. Adam was created before Eve, and she was created to be a supporter to him. Adam was given dominion over the world and everything in it. The animals were under his command, and he named them and gave them permission to live under his rule and reign. The world has remained in that order ever since. Women eventually claimed the respect that was due to them from generations past. A woman has always been the giver. She is the bearer of life. She is the nurturer and the caretaker. She is the backbone, the breath, and the life of a household. She is the glue that holds everything together. In general when a child is sick or crying, he wants his mother, not his father. There is something about her that brings healing to anything she touches. She feels out of place when she's on the receiving end because she's so accustomed to giving. That is why men should lead with love. If a man decides to treat his woman like a queen before expecting to be treated like a king, the relationship dynamic will run smoothly. If a woman serves a man selflessly first, he is likely to kick his feet up on his throne and continue ruling her. He may be gracious at times and reciprocate when it's convenient, but most often he will be lazy and continue taking. I am not leaving myself out of this example. I have lived this truth and watched it play out in my work countless times. This is based on data and experience, not just an idea.

As a man begins his selfless journey, he sets things in motion for the relationship to follow. He opens doors. He provides food and clothing to his household. He helps with the children. He helps in the kitchen before and/or after meals. He touches his wife's mind, her heart, and then her body. He gives to her and leaves it up to her to reciprocate his love. He doesn't force anything. He rests in his gentleness because he is strongest there. He speaks gently. He is slow to anger. He gives before he asks. He doesn't keep count of his blessings to her; he just is. That self-lessness sets the tone of the relationship. If he has chosen the right woman, it will press upon her heart to receive his love gladly but also to return his love in her own way.

A woman's selflessness will speak much louder to the man. Her love is the original creation of love because love is her calling. He has made love his duty and his honor, but she was born for love and shaped in its image. Her love will knock his socks off. He will not know what hit him. This reinforcing love will send the relationship into a cycle that is unstoppable. In this cycle, all purity is found. It's in this type of relation-ship where past pains are healed and everything is made new. The man becomes a new man, and the woman becomes a new woman. This love isn't about how much we can get but how much we can give.

It should be a challenge to see who can treat their spouse the best, but without keeping score. If you can remember everything you've done for your spouse, you're not being selfless. If you can list and name every act of kindness, you're not doing enough. If you mention in conversa-tion all you've done for your spouse, you're not being selfless. You're being selfish. From this day forward, be truly selfless. Don't mention your good deeds. There is no need to rub them in your spouse's face. They know exactly what you do for them. They may not mention it be-cause they know that in a matter of a couple days, you will be blowing your little horn from the mountaintops. They don't thank you enough because that would make two of you thanking you. They can't thank you more than or better than you thank yourself, so they've decided to re-main quiet. It's not that your spouse doesn't know your worth, it's that they know you've already overvalued yourself, so they leave their sticker price off. Be quiet with your mouth and let your actions speak louder.

Do more. Give more. Love more. Don't keep score. Don't mention your good deeds and see how long it takes for your spouse to mention them. When you are praised for all of your hard work, graciously accept your accolades and then get back to work. Don't bask in your glory for too long. You have work to do, and it's selfless.

You will notice after a while if your spouse appreciates your efforts. If you are married, well, then, you will have raised the bar in your relationship and the quality of your life will increase. Your life will become so blissful that it will feel like a fairy tale. It will feel so good to be in a competition of love.

There is no cookie-cutter guide to selflessness in your relationship. Each relationship may look different. In my household, it may mean that I wash the dishes after my wife cooks and then massage her feet when we get in bed. In another household, it may mean that the husband cooks dinner and then gives the kids a bath. Each relationship may look different. Love in the way you know will speak to your spouse. Don't try to emulate what you see online or in a movie. Do what you know your spouse needs from you.

The amount of pain and frustration you have caused your spouse will determine how long she expects your acts of kindness before reciprocating. Don't get weary or upset. If you've put your spouse through a lot, she may just kick her feet up for a month and accept the new love you're giving. If you married well, trust and know that eventually her tank will be full and she will reciprocate with love. Once you have made your spouse feel whole again, feel free to love selflessly and let this way of life be the new normal. Love doesn't have an expiration date. Love doesn't take breaks. Love is a job you can't retire from. You have to get up, put your work boots on, and go to work every day. There are no vacations from love. You don't have to slave or serve physically every day, but in every way, you must express love. It may be in your speech today and in your physical actions tomorrow. It shouldn't look the same every day. You are not a robot, nor are you a slave. Loving isn't hard, but it's not lazy either. You have to love selflessly day in and day out.

Love takes turns loving the lovers. Today may be your day, and tomorrow will be the other person's day. A relationship filled with selfless love will read like a fairy tale because most people are simply not accustomed to that type of two-way love. She may wake up before he does and cook breakfast from the fresh groceries he went to the store to buy the previous night. Then he wakes up, eats breakfast, and takes out the trash. Then she feeds the kids and loads them in the car for school and he drives them to school to save her some time. Then he texts her love notes throughout the day, and she returns the love. Then she gets home and cooks dinner for the family. He comes home, gets the kids ready for practice, and helps them with their homework. He takes the little athletes to practice, and they come home to a hot meal. After dinner, he washes the dishes, while she gets the kids ready for bed. After the kids are in bed, the couple watch television while he rubs her feet. After he rubs her feet, she moves in a little closer and begins to massage his back. They watch their favorite show and discuss their day. That's a day of selfless love. The next day, the roles could completely switch. No matter the day, both parties are doing what needs to be done. No one is keeping score. No one is pointing the finger with blame. They are just living and loving. I didn't dream up that day—I just recited one of my days. That's how selfless love feels. Selfless love heals. It wipes your worries away. Whatever you were stressing about is eased in the arms of love. Your mind can rest easy because your body is relaxed with love. It's service, but it doesn't feel like work. You could do these jobs for a living, but here you don't need any pay. The feeling they create is priceless, and you wouldn't trade it for the world. No amount of money can buy selfless love. This is what every relationship should be made of.

If you're keeping score, you're missing out on love, and you're losing the game anyway. It should be fun, not tedious and bothersome. You should be at ease, not in a ball of anxiety. If you practice loving this way, it will become second nature. You won't have to think about it. Her needs will be your commands. His wants will be your way.

If you've loved selflessly for longer than you can count and there is no reciprocation, you have a reason to worry. Selfless love must be a two-way street. If you're sending love out, it must come back. This type of love works like an investment. The love you give comes with a return. You aren't counting it, but you are subconsciously expecting it. The return of love is what fills you up, as you love with all of you. If there is no return, that means you're selflessly loving the wrong person or you're doing too little too late. That is when you must take inventory of your relationship and see if there is any mutual love left. It is possible to invest in the wrong person. It is also possible to hurt a person so much that your love loses its value. It is usually one of those two things to explain why the love you're giving is not coming back. Love is an action word. When you take action in love, it should be returned with equal or greater effort. If the return is lacking, the love is gone. It's then you must make a decision to love until it is awakened in your spouse or to step back and reassess the situation. Remember, I believe in making it work, but you can't make the wrong situation work. There has to be mutual love, or the relationship is void of all love.

Pay attention to love. You can pay attention without keeping score of your good deeds. If there is no love, don't ignore that fact. That's something you have to see. As you give of yourself, never lose yourself. Always give from a glad and whole heart. Always expect the same in return. There is a difference between giving to receive and giving with expectation of a return; the former has motives, but the latter has standards.

Here are some things to think about:

1. Are you a selfless lover? Be honest with yourself.

2. Have you ever loved and not received love in return? If yes, what did it do to your self-esteem?

3. How long can you love a person without receiving love in return?

4. Are you willing to love a person the way he or she needs to be loved instead of the way you want to love?

5. Are you the leader in love or the reciprocator?

6. Does this chapter on love make you want to change the effort you make, or are you right on track?

7. Do you believe people love differently? If so, do you believe you should at least be able to feel the love?

8. Are you willing to speak up if you aren't being loved in return?

9. Have you ever been hurt so much that the other person's love came too little, too late?

10. Does love come naturally to you, or do you need to learn how to love better?

seven

MIND YOUR OWN BUSINESS

Your relationship is like a house. You must build on a firm foundation. You must lock your doors to keep strangers out. You must mow your lawn so you can see the snakes. You must install fire alarms so you don't get trapped in a burning house. You must pay your dues.

Most people don't treat their relationship like a house. Many couples air their dirty laundry on Facebook. Some take their private business to work. Some open up a discussion in the barbershop or salon. Relationship drama will happen, but it gets much worse when it's open to so many outside opinions. To the best of your ability, your business needs to remain in-house. In-house business discussions should include a trusted professional. A trusted professional may not be a person volunteering his or her time at the church. Disclosing your business to that person might be opening you up to gossip in other circles. The trusted professional should be thoroughly vetted and someone who is bound by confidentiality. Outside of that, your business is between you and your spouse.

The number one offense is telling others the petty stuff. Your partner will not do everything to your liking. Men may leave their underwear on the floor or their dirty dinner plate on the table from time to time. Women may occasionally forget to wrap and conceal a used tampon in the trash next to the toilet. He may break wind on the couch while you're watching Netflix. Your spouse may wake up on the wrong side of the bed most mornings and need twenty to thirty minutes before holding a conversation. She may want to talk about something he has no interest in. He may want to discuss only his interests. On a lot of days, your spouse may annoy you 50 percent of the day. It's important that you weigh the matter. What is it that you don't like? How bad is it? Is it a deal breaker? Is it forcing you to lower your standards? Are you losing yourself to self-hate? Is it taking years off of your life? If it's not ruining your life, don't stress over it. What good does it do to take those petty complaints to the gossip circle? Who can fix those small problems? Who even cares about those small problems? Taking your business to the street is only opening your relationship up to more scrutiny and attacks from the enemy. As you focus on those small things, they become big things. Every second you give your attention to little things, you are feeding the issue. A small problem will continue to grow, and before you know it, it will become a giant one. You will begin to resent your spouse for no good reason. You will resent the humanness in your partner. But you have to remember that you are with a human, not a robot. Humans have quirky habits that will get on your nerves. As long as your self-worth and self-respect aren't being compromised, you're in good shape.

There will be some bigger issues that arise. There may be some arguments that get intense. There may be some sleepless nights because your blood pressure is a little high from the disagreement. Some nights, one person may take the couch. You may go a full day without speaking to your spouse. Certain issues may be fundamental issues that need addressing. How do you handle them?

Another problem couples have is running business back to Mom and Dad. Yes, your parents have acquired wisdom from life, but they are also family that loves you. Pay attention to your discussions with your family members. How often do you brag about all the amazing qualities your spouse possesses? How often do you talk about all their flaws? In most cases, you spend more time griping and complaining about their shortcomings. Remember, it's you, not Mom and Dad, who is in love with your spouse. You can gripe about your spouse and then feel good because you've dumped the complaints on someone else. Now you're back on good terms with your spouse, but Mom and Dad hold on to those complaints. You're their beloved child. Mom and Dad want the best for you. You sounded very unhappy and frustrated. Oh, no! You're not living the fairy-tale love story that you always dreamed of having—Mommy to the rescue. Now Mommy is coming over more often and giving your spouse the evil side-eye. You're bubbly and happy because you're over the petty stuff you once complained about, but Mom remembers it.

Imagine if this happens every week; Mom will have had it up to her eyeballs with your spouse, while you're just fine. There's something weird in the air. Everyone wants to have a good time, but there's tension in the house. Perhaps there was supposed to be a nice, relaxing family get-together, but something feels off. It totally slipped your mind that you ran your lover's name into the ground thirty minutes a day for seven days straight the previous week. That was your therapy, but your mom and dad are not therapists. They didn't leave the drama in the therapy room. They've come for Bobby's head. They can't take it off, so they'll just glare at him and let him catch them glaring a few times when you're not looking. Oh, he feels it. It's burning him up. He feels eyes on the back of his neck, then on his forehead, and he just can't get comfortable. It's all because you tried to make your parents your therapist and it backfired.

There are some parents who can listen to their child's relationship problems, give advice, and not hold a grudge against their son- or daughter-in-law, but that is very rare. Even in those cases, the advice starts to get one-sided. Yes, your parents may not show any signs of anger toward your spouse, but if you pay attention, their advice to you is usually in your favor. It's natural for parents to be biased toward their own child, but it leaves you feeling that you're in the right 90 percent of the time. That's not healthy for your relationship because you never get to see yourself through the eyes of your spouse. You aren't perfect any more than he or she is. You just get to hear how perfect you are from a parent who adores you but doesn't have to share a bed and a house with you.

Imagine both parties having gripe sessions with their parents every week. Imagine the tension. Imagine the separation. Think about the family events and the stares being passed around the room. When it's time to pray, there are subliminal shots being taken in the prayer at the other family. The Thanksgiving prayer begins to sound like a battle rap instead of a moment of gratitude before God. Complaints from December 1 of last year up until the Thanksgiving prayer have been piling up. Oh, it's go time. The other side of the family is going to hear about this before Jesus himself. Something has to be done about their child and the lack of manners from their upbringing. The prayer sounds like "Father, help everyone to see his or her own faults. Whether it's starting arguments daily or not seeing the value in their spouse. Help a special some-one see the error of their ways. Today we are grateful for the blessings you've put in our lives. Not everyone realizes how blessed they are, with the spouse they've been given. Help them today, Lord, Amen."

Couples put their families at war every day, stemming from little spiteful conversations that should have never been had. Of course you shouldn't bottle up everything you feel, but that's why communication with your spouse is so important. You can't communicate with everyone else and then expect your spouse to read your mind. You have to be open with your feelings and keep your business in-house.

This really isn't easy to do. It's one of the hardest things to do the right way. There is a right way to do it, but it's not something you want to hear. Telling your best friend isn't the way to go, either. At times, best friends can be worse than parents. It's not just about the arguments. Sometimes couples tell their best friends about their intimate moments. Your business is for you, not your best friends. There have been millions of affairs created by the curiosity of a best friend. I've coached countless couples who set themselves up for failure by bragging about the bed-room to a best friend. You have to be careful about whom you call a friend. There are good friends, and there are those who pretend to be a good friend, but all the while they want what you have. It's especially dangerous if your friend isn't happy in his or her own relationship. You can really set yourself up for problems.

We are all human. If you tell a human a descriptive story about your intimate life with your spouse, that person will not forget. Not only will he or she not forget, but he or she also will never see your spouse the same way. Your relationship won't always be perfect, and during the tough or weakened states, there will be room for a fake friend to move in on your spouse. Your best friend is not your therapist, either. Your best friend should not be the therapist to your spouse. Your best friend should not be consulting or advising your spouse on matters that deal with you. Your spouse should not be in contact with your best friend unless everyone involved knows about the conversations. So-called friends ruin many marriages. At this very moment, many affairs are happening with supposed best friends. This is not common sense, nor is it even fathomable to many.

Not only should you keep your intimate business from your best friend, but you also can't make a habit of sharing the details of your arguments with your best friend. Your friend is biased. Unlike your parents, it's not your friend's dream for you to be happily married. Your friend may be just fine with you being divorced so you can be available to them more often. To a certain degree, marriage has caused your friend to experience somewhat of a loss. Your friend misses you, and the one-sided advice you get when speaking to your friend is a testament of that fact. The next time you share your relationship business with a friend, pay close attention to the advice given to you. Listen to the pattern of advice. If it's always in your favor and you know your spouse is not a bad person, that's a sign the advice you're getting isn't the best. It is not to say your friend is a bad person, either. Your friend cares for you and wants you to be happy. Your friend knows if they don't say what you want to hear, you may cut them off, but you won't cut off your lover. They are trying to tell you what you want to hear because they don't want to lose you. Friends know that no tie is stronger than the soul tie you have with a lover. They don't want to be on the losing end. They will feed you what it seems you can digest. You have to be careful with how much you take in because it could be detrimental to your relationship.

If you can't afford the help of a professional and books just aren't doing enough for you, then yes, you have to talk to someone. There is a way to do it. You have to be up front about your own flaws and short-comings, too. Disclose the real stuff you say and do to your spouse. Tell it from their perspective, too. You've heard their perspective on you in your disagreements. Repeat them to the person whom you tell all your business to. You also have to tell all the amazing things your spouse does. Highlight each and every effort that you have been so conveniently leaving out. Level the playing field. Then see what your confidant does with this new and balanced information. Hear what they have to say, and then weigh it with your heart. You're not a dummy. You didn't get this far in life and have the wisdom to read this book if you're not intelligent. Deep down, you know the answers. It may not be what you want to hear, but you know the truth of the matter.

In this day and time, with social media being so prevalent, it is ruining a lot of relationships. You can't allow social media to be your therapist, either, because not every post applies to your current situation. I can attest to the dangers of social media. I have coached many people who told me they made life-altering decisions based on their interpretation of one of my posts. People have both stayed in relationships and ended relationships due to my posts. As I listen to their interpretation of what I wrote, in most cases, the person is completely wrong about the meaning of my message. It's natural for our minds to make what we read mean something to us. We will take things out of context because we are desperate for advice. I know this. I can't shut up online because of it, but I'm a lot more careful about my posts now because of this. You can't believe everything you read, because you don't know where it's coming from. Someone's mom who is fighting a terminal disease could have inspired the post, but you apply it to your relationship and the interpretation is wrong. The post could be inspired by someone's career goals, but you apply it to your toxic relationship and the interpretation nearly gets you killed. Don't let a meme on social media decide the outcome of your relationship.

On the other side of the social media issue is couples posting subliminal or very blatant messages directed at their spouse on Facebook. Most of us have done it. Why do we do it? We are seeking validation and approval for our way of thinking. We are hoping that our spouse will see the post and then see the comments from people agreeing with us. We want that person to feel guilty or wrong for what they've done. It's really a form of cyberbullying. You can make your spouse feel worthless by beating them up on social media. You're airing dirty laundry, but none of it is yours. You're letting people look at your partner's soiled underwear online and everyone is commenting about how disgusting and gross he or she is. Think about it like that. Posting a one-sided argument on social media is not fair to your spouse or to your relationship as a whole. You are hurting yourself and setting yourself up for failure. People will say what you want to hear, in most cases, and your point will be proven, temporarily. It becomes a nightmare if your partner decides to retaliate next week. Now their fake friends on Facebook are cheering them on and are in their corner. Both of you are quarreling in a very childish way by using social media to fight your battles. It's like polling the audience to decide what you should do in your home. Sadly, even the most successful and sophisticated people have resorted to this form of coercion in their relationships. It is toxic and dangerous. Imagine knocking your spouse to the ground and kicking them in their private area. Then imagine inviting ten to a hundred strangers to kick them in the privates, too. Really picture that. Would you do that to them? To post private issues on a public site is humiliating both to your spouse and to your relationship. Nearly everyone has done it, so everyone knows what it looks like. No one is stupid. You tell yourself that maybe people think you are speaking hypothetically and no one knows that it's really referring to your relationship. That is what you'd like to believe. Everyone knows what you're talking about, and now everyone has lost respect for you and your union. Keep your business in-house.

It is no better to discuss your private matters in the church group, the work group, or any group. Your business is your business, and if you let untrained humans in who have no credentials or certifications to give you advice, you are inviting disaster to visit your home. People speak from where they are. You have no clue what a person is dealing with behind closed doors. You may be open enough to share your business with them, but they'll never share their business with you. Yet, because you asked, they will speak to your situation from their brokenness. Their brokenness can further break your situation.

Talk to God first. Search the scriptures and see how you should love. Ephesians 5 is my favorite when learning about marriage. I consider forgiveness, compassion, and understanding. All of those things must be taken into account.

Create your circle of influence. Yes, you should treat your relationship like a house, but you can't get trapped in a burning house. You must have the alarms working properly so you can be notified when there is smoke. Put the fire out fast. To do that, you have to have a plan in place. You can consult the scriptures first. Then have a levelheaded conversation with your spouse. Both of you must be open to reason. You can solve 90 percent of your problems without ever setting foot outside your house. For the things you can't solve, get outside help.

What should the help look like? The help should be a professional, not a family member or a friend. Most professionals join this line of work for the same reason, to help people. A Google search for a family therapist will bring up a list of local options. Look at their reviews if they have them. If three are available, identify the top three and set up a consult with them. Make sure you don't know the person and the person does not attend your church or know you in any way. Interview them and ask what areas he or she wants to focus on. Ask them why they do this work. Ask them how they got into this work. Ask them if they also have personal experience with marriage issues or if it's just the knowledge they've gained from school. Ask them if they also consider themselves a life coach as well as a therapist.

The goal is to find someone who helps couples because it's their passion, not just their profession. A person doesn't need extensive personal experience, but it's a plus if he or she does have some personal experience. No matter how amazing their answers are, always remember that you're dealing with a human being. All humans are capable of error. Talk to the professional. Air your grievances. Have individual sessions as well as couples sessions. From my experience, I recommend individual sessions first. It's important to be able to tell your side of things without holding back. Let your spouse do the same. The professional will be able to call it straight down the middle. The professional will tell each of you what you need to work on and give you some tips on how to do so. Both of you have to come back into the relationship and do the work. Don't share what you learned with your spouse, because it's for you. Don't discuss with your spouse what you discuss with the therapist, because that's your private session. You don't want to come home and start an argument without a referee. Just come home and do the work with a smile—

service with a smile. That has to be the goal of both parties. Just do the work. After two to four individual sessions, you can try one or two sessions together. If the session turns into a fight, it's not time for sessions together just yet. If counseling makes things worse before they get better, that's normal. Just keep that in mind and keep getting better.

It's important to go to a professional because this stuff isn't common sense. If it were common sense, every relationship would be perfect. It takes real knowledge to make a relationship work. I know a lot of people say they don't want anyone in their business. Well, if you can't make it right on your own, you need someone in your business. At least let that someone be someone qualified to give advice. Let that someone be someone who is unbiased and wants to help. It's worth the price you'll pay. It's their profession; pay them. You want to be paid at work; well, so do they. This is an investment in your relationship. If the relationship isn't worth investing in, it's not worth being in.

If a friend or family member is a coach or therapist, you can visit that person if it's the only option you have. Something is better than nothing. You both have to be okay with someone you know being privy to all of your in-house secrets. If either of you is uncomfortable with that, it's not an option. Find someone else, and make the investment. If you can't afford it, watch every YouTube video I have posted, read every book you can afford, and talk to each other with love until you can afford it. Remember, a professional is an entrepreneur. He or she will quote you a price, but feel free to tell him or her what you can afford. Most will accept what you can afford to pay. I don't think any will accept less than $25 per hour, but the normal price is around $100 per hour. If you have to skip going out to eat to afford it, do it. If you have to turn off your cable to afford it, do it.

Nothing is more important than love other than food, water, and oxygen. You have a fighting chance, save it!

Not talking to friends and family about your spouse in a negative way is a practice you must try. The act of not complaining about small things will create more peace and happiness in your life. If you pray about it and take action instead of complaining about it, you may not need to hire a professional. Make it a habit and a practice not to complain to anyone about your spouse. Knock your friends' and families' socks off by never again speaking ill of your spouse. Don't feed your spirit negativity. Don't dwell on pain points. Dwell on healing. What you focus on is magnified. Magnify peace, healing, and growth. The more you talk about problems, the more problems you'll have. The more you talk about solutions, the more you'll generate.

Keep your business in-house, and watch the difference it makes. I do not mean sit in a burning house. I mean, if it's not worth breaking up over, it's not worth fighting over. We get a feeling when something is seriously wrong in a relationship. When things are very toxic, we have to tell someone who will listen. It's smart to have an ally on the outside if things are toxic on the inside. One mistake people make is keeping quiet when things are dangerous behind closed doors. That's a mistake you don't want to make. If things are so toxic that your safety and sanity are at risk, tell friends and family and be on your way out of that relationship. It's the small, petty, insignificant things that most couples turn into big problems and ruin their relationship. Know the difference, and don't make excuses for yourself one way or the other.

Listen to your heart. Treat your relationship like a house, but never get trapped in a burning one.

Here are some things to think about:

1. Treat your relationship like your house!

2. How much of your business do you share inappropriately?

3. Have you told too much of your business to fix it?

4. Can you move forward focusing on the positives and not gossiping about the negatives?

5. Do you need to hit the reset button with your friends and family to keep them on the outside of your relationship instead of on the inside?

6. Have you ever hired a professional to help you in your relationship? If not, why?

7. Do you think your spouse would be open to outside help?

8. If your spouse doesn't want to work on the relationship, would you leave it?

9. Do you have any experiences you wish you had kept in-house?

10. What things do you feel are necessary to tell friends and family?

eight

BE FAITHFUL

It seems so simple and easy to understand when you are told to be faithful. For some people, it's a walk in the park. For a lot of others, it can get pretty complex. Being faithful isn't easy in a world of lies and misdirection. Loyalty isn't something we hold near and dear to our hearts. It's survival of the fittest. We want the latest and greatest version of everything. Why aren't you faithful to your job? Why aren't you faithful to your smartphone? Why aren't you faithful to your car? Why aren't you faithful to your gym? Why aren't you faithful to social media? We aren't taught to be faithful anymore. What will serve you best in this stage of your life? That's what you want. It shouldn't be that way in relationships, but oftentimes it is. Many people want the latest version of lovers. The body type in style is who you want to lie next to. The height requirement must be met. How is the smile looking these days? Can the person you love afford a new smile to fix their crooked one? Does he or she have the discipline to have an eight-pack of abs? We turn our backs on anything and everything. We know we can't trade in our parents and siblings, but nearly everything else is interchangeable in our society. There is so much variety that it's hard to be satisfied. Facebook shows us a news feed of options. Television bombards us with commercials of options. Instagram teases us with popular pages. Twitter has a timeline to steal all your time. There are so many options to choose from daily. How can you choose one? How can you remain faithful when there's a different flavor every month? We are constantly shown other options that appear to be better than the one we have.

There are men online who appear to be the perfect husbands. There are women online who seem to have it all, and they can cook. There are guys who are tall, muscular, handsome, build stuff for the house, fix stuff around the house, make great money, and have the right number of teeth for a killer smile. The women have great abs, perfect thighs, and perfect smiles, make great money, and have their mommy duties in order, and their homes always seem to be clean. Social media show us not what we need to see but what we want to believe. That makes it hard to be faithful in today's society.

Think back to the days prior to social media. Life was so much simpler. There was so much more time to go around. Think back to before there were so many cable networks and shows to choose from. We had more time for family conversations and game nights. Couples had time to talk, laugh, and fall deeper in love. Now couples rush home to eat fast food and scroll down a timeline comparing their reality to someone else's highlight reel. This lifestyle is stealing joy, peace, and happiness. It's hard to look at your spouse and be content if you're comparing him or her to the outer appearance of everyone you see online. You see what people show you, and you believe it! You don't consider that you can't believe half of what you see online. Did you ever stop to consider that it's all lies? What if other people's behind-the-scenes are worse than yours? It's a strong possibility that their situation is just as bad as, if not worse than, yours. As a life coach, I'm behind the scenes often. I don't believe my own hype, so I definitely don't believe the hype of others. I've always been a realist, but my line of work has helped me become even more of one than ever before. We see millionaires who seem to have it all go into foreclosure on their homes. How did that happen? It happened because what you can see is not their reality. Your perception is your reality but not theirs. To be faithful, you first have to realize that the grass is rarely greener on the other side. Stop comparing your situation for a second, and be content. Work on your relationship, and be happy where you are. If you give your relationship the time and attention it deserves, you'll see very quickly that happiness is your choice.

Many people think being faithful means not having sex with anyone else. It goes much deeper than that. Lovemaking isn't actually sex; it's conversation. We don't fall in love through sex. We fall in love through communication. If you're spending four hours each day talking to someone you work with, you will build love for that person. If it's someone you can actually be intimate with, it's even more dangerous. That's where the term *work wife* comes from. There are also "work husbands." It seems harmless in theory, but it's very dangerous in reality. To be faithful means to be faithful in mind, body, and spirit. If you are confiding in someone you can develop feelings for, you are taking a big risk that could cost you greatly. I know you want to claim that it's innocent, but it's not. It may begin innocently, but eventually it will manifest into something much greater. Conversation leads to love. Love comes after lust. The lust can really burn you. You have to be very careful what you're entertaining. The person you're dealing with at work or online may have hidden motives. That person could have come into the friendship with a goal to steal your heart and you never saw it coming. The initial innocence of the conversation is to make you drop your guard. Once your guard is dropped, he or she can move in for the capture or sow confusion within your heart. In most cases it happens before you even realize it. Sometimes it was neither party's intention to fall into sex sin. Both parties really thought it was a work relationship. The conversation seemed innocent and productive with a common goal at hand. They thought it was about work, but it turned out to be more. Before you know it, someone's heart begins to change. It's very dangerous when both hearts begin to change at the same time. The conversation is filling a void. It's reminding you of the times you've built innocent and pure love with someone. It feels new. It feels fresh. It feels like what you need. You don't want to call it love, but you begin to fantasize about the person's conversation. You think about that person when he or she isn't around, and you can't wait to get back to work or online to talk more. It's getting dangerous. The conversation is no longer innocent. Now it serves a purpose, and that purpose is going to ruin your relationship.

We never see it coming if it wasn't our intention. In fact, sometimes it may take years before things turn for the worst. There are some people who will read this right now and say they have a friend at work or online who is completely innocent and they've been talking for years. That may be true, but it doesn't mean that in another year, or maybe even two, a turn won't happen. It's walking on dangerous ground. In the thousands of cases that have come across my desk, I have never seen it play out well. It always ends up messy in one way or another.

Before the sex is just the communication. This is where the emotional cheating starts. Emotional cheating can be worse than physical cheating. Emotional cheating is so dangerous because you're building love instead of fulfilling lust. To fulfill lust is to have sex. If you have sex with someone you've just met, there are no feelings involved. It still affects you and you sin against your body, but it's easier to sweep it under the rug and move on, until you trip over your mess later. If you've been emotionally cheating and then it builds to sex, it's pretty much over for your relationship. There have been many cases where an affair led to a divorce and the person who was caught cheating ends up marrying the person in the affair. This happens because there is a false sense of love and security that is formed during an affair. In those instances, you are able to build with a person without all the day-to-day drama that comes with a relationship. You give that person your best, and you get his or her best in return. The junk in between is given to the person at home, who is clueless about the affair.

This is why the work buddy or online buddy seems to be so perfect. This is why you start comparing your partner to this person you're talking to every day. This is why it seems that your partner just isn't matching up. This happens because you're not seeing the flaws of the person you're emotionally cheating with; you're getting the perfect version of this person, not the real person. It's false, but you make it your reality. Before you know it, you'll be arguing with your spouse every day because you're having withdrawals from your other lover. Yes, the person is your other lover because you're building love with him or her. It's being built on a false foundation that may fall from beneath you at some point, but it's being built nonetheless. This happens every day. The workplace or social media become a breeding ground for affairs that will ruin all the lives involved.

The dynamics of cheating can be very complex. The person you call a friend can actually be a lover, and the person you call your lover can actually be your foe. This all unfolds as you're going through the motions with your "work wife" or "work husband." It develops right under your nose, and you never sniff it. Then, one day, it's fully matured and it punches you in the nose. Wow, how life comes at you fast! Some of the best marriages have been ruined by a seemingly innocent friendship started at work.

Every relationship has problems. I've never heard of a perfect relationship without a single problem. It doesn't exist. Even if things are moving along smoothly, problems are on the way. Things can be going great for you while unraveling for the friend you're confiding in at work. Your intentions can be pure. But your work buddy has issues at home, and so you start to look more amazing. You may not be fantasizing about your friend, but he or she is fantasizing about you. Then one day, a conversation about your spouse's strengths and weaknesses will come up. The person you're talking to daily will just happen to be strong in every area in which your spouse falls short. Wow, what a surprise. Now your innocence is intrigued. Could you have found your soul mate who has been cast as a friend? Probably not, but it sure will look that way.

There are so many angles and directions from which cheating can sneak up on you. No matter how sneaky the attack, we ultimately cheat by choice—not by chance. Before you go all the way, there will be a fork in the road. You can go toward safety, or you can go toward destruction. Yes, sometimes people meet someone who could be better for them than the person they married. But the person they meet shouldn't be the bridge to divorce. A healthy relationship should never begin with an affair. That faulty foundation will cost you every time without fail.

Faithfulness must be a priority. It must be the main focus and the goal of every relationship. It's a nonnegotiable factor. You must be faithful. Faithfulness means that you have set boundaries. Certain things must be sacred, and you can't mix the sacred with the profane. You must be faithful not only in deed but also in appearance. That means you have to think twice before going to a meeting one-on-one with someone you could potentially fall for or even appear to be falling for. You may say in your heart that it's impossible, but if it looks possible to others, you're still being unfaithful. As stated in Romans 14:16, "Let not your good be evil spoken of."

Being faithful is not hard if you make a serious effort to do so. There are things that must be reserved for your spouse only. They may be one-on-one outings. They may be phone conversations after a certain hour of the night. They may be certain words, terms, or phrases. They may be certain acts of kindness. Is it appropriate for a man to call his wife and a woman he works with by the same term of endearment? Is it appropriate for a woman to be on the phone with another man at 10 p.m.? Is it appropriate for a man to go out of town to a conference alone with another woman? There must be boundaries. No boundaries are too strict or unreasonable if they work for you and your marriage. One man may say he doesn't want to speak on the phone with another woman unless his wife is present. That's perfectly reasonable if he knows that will hold him accountable. A woman may say she doesn't want to speak to a man in person alone. That's perfectly reasonable if that's what makes her feel comfortable. There must be boundaries in place. As a couple you have to establish those boundaries within reason. If you don't agree with your spouse's boundaries, speak up. Evaluate the reasoning behind the boundaries the other person is asking of you. Boundaries should not equate to prison. A relationship should not make you feel like you're in prison, and you've committed no crime. That's abuse, and that can't be tolerated. If you know in your heart that the boundaries are fair and you can understand the reasoning behind them, abide by them. It's in your best interest and the best interest of your relationship. The boundaries you're asked to keep may feel imposing or seem unfair if you've already been caught cheating. That's a price you have to pay to rebuild the trust. As long as you're not being abused in any way, give that reassurance to help rebuild your relationship.

To be honest, most people who cheat wanted to cheat. It's not uncommon for people to set themselves up to cheat. An affair can be a rush of excitement to some people. Depending on a person's background, upbringing, and experiences, he or she may find cheating to be a thrill. But it's very dangerous. Lives are taken due to infidelity. Families are broken up and children are damaged due to infidelity. It's one of society's biggest problems, and we must be more diligent in our efforts to prevent it, not just for ourselves but also when we see friends and family stepping out of line. Sometimes that unsolicited advice is needed. It will ring loudly when their head hits the pillow. Saving our relationships will save our world. We need more faithful couples. It's not just a problem for men. There are millions of women who cheat in their relationships, too.

For men, cheating had been a dilemma from the beginning of time. For women, it may have happened but we've never heard of it. Men might admit when they cheat on their woman but never tell when they cheat with someone else's woman. I was shocked to learn that women also cheat. I learned this in my coaching practice, and it blew me away. We've been conditioned to expect men to cheat at some time. I don't meet many faithful men. I do meet faithful men, but not nearly as many as cheating men. We have created the "zero and the hero" theory when it comes to cheating. To men, a cheating man is a hero and a cheating woman is a zero. To women, a cheating man is a zero, but if she stays with him, she's telling him he's a hero. For a lot of cheating men, the infidelity has no reason. A man may cheat on a woman he loves. It doesn't make any sense, but it is true. It's true only because there are different levels of love and different types of love. In the moments that love isn't an action, it is reduced to a feeling. In the moment of infidelity, a man blocks his feelings of love for his woman and gives in to his desires for pleasure. He gives in to his nature that was created to procreate. He hasn't evolved and matured into the man he is supposed to become, and he's acting out of immaturity, greed, and lust. The urge in his wiring is so strong that without a deep-rooted conviction to combat the feeling, he falls into the trappings of pleasure over and over again. It's an excuse if you want it to be. Yes, it is pitiful, despicable, and every other name you can call it, but it's reality. If a human has no conviction, he or she has no boundaries. Men cheat for reasons we can't often articulate. After more than a decade of coaching these men, I've come to that conclusion. I've also been that man in my youth, and I had to deeply evaluate my reasoning, and the findings are so trivial that it's baffling. Men who cheat are filling a void, just as women who cheat are filling a void. The voids may be completely different. For the most part, both sexes are trying to fill voids of validation, affirmation, and appreciation. Those voids may be from parents, or they could be from the current relationship. To cheat is to admit that something is wrong with you internally. Cheating is a vile act. It doesn't come easy, and if you do it and make it easy, that's a dangerous sign.

My findings have taught me that women cheat for a couple of main reasons. The most common reason is that a woman is with a "hold-me-over" man. This man isn't the man she wants—he's just the man she has. He's not the right man or the right look, or his bank account isn't the right size. She's waiting on Mr. Right, but this guy is Mr. Right Now. He's Mr. Right Now because she's too broken internally to be alone while in waiting. She needs a guy to hold her over. It's easy to justify her actions in her mind because the man is probably a jerk anyway. Most guys are jerks at some point in the relationship, and this type of woman will really make him pay for it. There are also men who are perfect in the relationship yet still fall into the Mr. Right Now category and get cheated on when cheating is convenient. Typically, I notice these women have already been hurt so many times they aren't really looking for love anymore. They are looking for a man who can keep them financially stable. They have formed the mind-set that all men are dogs, so if he's going to chase the kitty around town, he needs to at least have money she can spend when she's angry with him for cheating. This mind-set is spreading like wildfire in our social media–run society. Everything is mixing together, and everything affects everything. Social media affect relationships in so many ways. This mind-set in women is increasingly growing, and a lot of women don't even realize they are a part of the problem. The guy is an okay choice until a better guy comes along. The better guy gets to cheat with this woman, and if he wants to make it official, the woman looks for the next opportunity to call off her current relationship with Mr. Right Now.

The second most common reason women cheat is that the relationship is dead but she hasn't left. Many women won't leave a dead relationship due to financial reasons or living arrangements. Instead of leaving, the woman will just decide to start seeing other men while her man is preoccupied with his other women. It seems very pointless to cheat in this way and some find it hard to even call it cheating, but it is. This may also be known as revenge cheating. Many women fall victim to this mentality that says they should think like a man, failing to realize that sleeping around with random men is not thinking like a man; it's thinking more like a grown-boy, not a grown man. Now this educated and very capable woman is emulating the lifestyle choices of a lost and immature man. She's perpetuating the cycle and hurting herself more than she's hurting him. The sad part is that sometimes a woman cheats and the man she is cheating on never finds out. In that case, it can't really be called revenge cheating. It really just hurts the woman's mind, body, and spirit. She's broken, just like the man she's trying to hurt with revenge.

For serial cheaters, changing may not be easy. It takes a lot to be faithful after promiscuity has become your lifestyle of choice. But it can be done. Yes, cheaters can change. It is not necessarily true that once a cheater, always a cheater. If a cheater has a deep enough reason to change, he or she can change. It takes conviction and commitment to change your cheating ways. It takes finding a deeper meaning in life and a connection with your purpose. For cheaters, love is not enough to remain faithful. It takes something stronger than romantic feelings for another person. Being faithful with your body is not enough. You have to be faithful in your mind and spirit as well. Many people don't cheat physically, but they cheat spiritually through pornography and masturbation. That's still cheating. It works against your relationship the same way cheating physically works against it. You will still compare your partner to others, and it will still affect your communication and chemistry. If you're giving your physical love to a phone or computer screen, you won't have the energy and focus you need for your spouse.

You have to connect on a deeper level with yourself. You have to give faithfulness a try. Try it wholeheartedly. You can make up your mind to be 100 percent faithful. You are strong enough to do it on your own will for a long period of time. Depending on your history with cheating, the definition of a long time will vary from person to person. For myself, I was able to rely on my own will to remain faithful for two years. After that, I needed the help of God. The help of God was granted because I prayed for the strength and the wisdom to be faithful.

Here's what happens when you're faithful. Being faithful increases your focus. You are able to focus on your dreams and goals with better concentration because in your free time, you are not entertaining outsiders. Being faithful increases your productivity. You produce so much more when you're focused and driven. Faithfulness also increases your happiness because you don't have to worry about others getting you out of your happy zone. You only have to focus on your spouse. Petty arguments and misunderstandings are avoided a lot more easily because your attention is focused on your spouse. Being faithful also brings peace. The need to check phones, emails, and social media inboxes begins to fade once trust is built. Not having to worry about a text or random call coming in at the wrong time makes things very peaceful and relaxed in your relationship. After these things are in place, the divine happens. Everything affects everything else, so if you're focused, happy, stress free, peaceful, and productive, you're naturally going to live a better life. You will begin to earn more money. You will gain more success in your business or on your job. Also, the favor of God will be in your life like never before because you've cleared the channel and God can reach you on the main line. He can reach you because your spirit is no longer cluttered with mess. The lies are out of the way. The deception is out of the way. The sex sin is out of the way. God can come into your heart and stay. He doesn't have to turn His head every time you enter the bathroom with your cell phone. He doesn't have to turn His head when you're surfing the Facebook inbox. He doesn't have to turn His head when you're at work with the potential work wives or work husbands. God can be present in your life and pour out blessings upon blessings. This is where the shift happens. Now you're making more money. You're tapping into your life's purpose, and, most important, you're pleasing in the sight of God. There is so much grace and favor in this space. It's a feeling you've never felt before, and it feels so amazing, you wouldn't trade it for the world. When you get out of your mess and you allow God to bless you, your life changes! Things don't happen to you the way they used to. Now, in the midst of trials, you're able to find rest. This is the favored life. With purpose and favor in your life, things become easier. The hard things feel easier. The tough times still look like blessed times. This is a feeling that not everyone gets to experience because not everyone is willing to sacrifice fleshly desires and live this lifestyle.

This is how cheaters become faithful. If you give yourself the chance to see the other side, you'll never want to step outside of God's favor and go back to the wilderness again. That's how I changed my life for good. I gave myself a chance, and then God stepped in and took the steering wheel. Not only am I faithful to my wife, I'm faithful to God. I'm faithful to God because it's His blessings and favor that changed my life. Yes, He is a graceful and merciful God, but His grace can't be taken for granted or it will cease to be granted. God will not be mocked, and the spirit of God is no fool. Good things won't come to bad people forever. Good things will eventually come to good people.

Give faithfulness and focus a try. Run your race, and when you're weak, lean on the everlasting arms of the Almighty. Be faithful to something bigger than yourself. It takes a combination of many things. Be faithful to God. Be faithful to yourself. Be faithful to your spouse. Be faithful to your purpose. Be faithful to your calling. You will be exalted so high in your life that you won't want to come back down. It will be clear that grace and favor got you there, but the work you did will also be clear. You will lose all desire to step outside of God's favor, and your cheating ways will be cured. It's a mind-set. It's a decision. It's a lifestyle.

Here are some things to think about:

1. Have you ever cheated? If so, why?

2. If you've never cheated, would you?

3. If you would never cheat, why not?

4. Have you ever been cheated on? If so, how did it make you feel?

5. If you think you've never been cheated on and find out that you have been, how would you handle it?

6. Faithfulness produces happiness.

7. Cheating doesn't mean something is wrong with your relationship; it means something is wrong with you.

8. Happy, faithful couples live longer, earn more money, and are healthier.

9. You don't cheat by chance, you cheat by choice.

10. Emotional cheating can be worse than physical cheating.

nine

FORGIVE AND FORGET

The saying "Forgive and forget" rolls off the tongue so easily, but to do it is a difficult task. In over a decade of coaching relationships I've never met a single person who forgot about his or her spouse's offenses. We don't forget. It's next to impossible to forget the things that hurt you in a relationship. For me, the saying doesn't mean exactly what it suggests. It's human to feel, to hurt, and to remember. Don't feel strange or like you're a terrible person because the offense plays over and over in your mind for months. It's normal. It's a process we all go through when we're hurt by someone we love. We go through the same process when someone we don't love hurts us. It's simply how the brain works. We remember every painful event. It is etched into our memory because the brain sensed it and began the process of healing our heart in response to it. Most people find a way to cope with the pain, even if they don't heal from it. Some are able to forget the pain and the offense and move on. Others allow the pain to cripple them and render them helpless for years after. You can't judge people by how they process their pain. It's their burden to bear. You can't dictate how and when they heal, especially if you're the one who caused the pain. Each of us has our own process of healing. It's up to me to heal my heart. It's up to you to heal your heart. You may be fortunate enough to have some assistance, but it's not always guaranteed. It may be a lonely journey to healing.

I've coached many people who are still in pain for years after the offense occurs. It's mind-boggling to me sometimes because the wrong-doing may not be that severe in my mind. It could be something as simple as a man being caught texting with another woman late at night. It's not right, but it's not something I would expect to sting for years. Yet we must consider a person's history with trauma and pain. Different people process things differently based on their life experiences. What doesn't hurt one person could crush another. That's why navigating the process of healing and forgiving is such a delicate issue. It takes time and tact.

We do not forget, but it is imperative that we forgive. How do you forgive? Forgiveness is just as much for you as it is for your spouse. Recently, I was coaching a client, and he spoke about forgiveness and how his decision to forgive had freed him. Holding on to the grudge was changing his personality and making him a different person. He felt drained, and it was painful to live in a bubble of anger all the time. So he decided to forgive, and it allowed him to return to his true self again. It confirmed in my spirit that forgiveness is something we do for ourselves as well. It's liberating. You have to do it on your own time, but also know that the longer you wait, the worse the relationship will get.

What is your motive for not forgiving? Is it to teach your spouse a lesson? Is it to drive a point home? Is it to protect yourself? Is it to prepare you for a breakup? Is it for sympathy? Is it for attention? Is it just because it's how you like feeling? That's an answer only you know. You have to be honest with yourself in order to find healing and forgiveness. I've seen many different scenarios play out. In the purest form of pain, you may not forgive because it hurts so badly and you are unable to bounce back right away. The next phase is protection. You may hold on to the pain to protect yourself from being hurt again. Perhaps you fear dropping your guard and suffering all over again. The next phase is to send a message and make a point about the offense. Here you are trying to let your spouse know that what they did is unacceptable and will not be tolerated. You are punishing your spouse and making them feel isolated so they'll think twice before ever hurting you again. The next phase is for sympathy. In this phase, you're able to get gifts, "I love you's," and a bunch of sweet nothings. You see a different side of your spouse if he or she is remorseful. This space can feel wonderful because you're getting attention that may not be common in your relationship. The next phase is resentment. In this phase you're just angry your partner had the audacity to hurt you. Your emotions have evolved from hurt to anger. Just the thought of what they did ticks you off. You hold on to the feeling just because. It feels good to be mad at someone for a little while because it tricks your mind into believing the anger is serving a purpose.

Those are the phases of forgiveness that I see most often. The individual couple and the reasons they are together usually determine which phase they spend the most time tackling. Then comes the choice to forgive, finally. At this point you have to consider the reason for the offense. Does it make sense? Is it acceptable? What I mean by this is that you have to look back over your partner's life. See if there are incidents in his or her life that led him or her to this point. Our history and biography make us who we are. What a person has lived through can determine who they become and how they behave in a relationship. Just seeking understanding of who they are as a person helps a lot in the forgiving process. The next thing you have to do is look at yourself and the role you played in the offense. Were you an innocent bystander? Were you doing everything in the relationship you were supposed to be doing? Or were you pushing the other person away, hurting them, or an antagonist in the situation?

There are times we are a part of the antecedent behavior that led to the offense. It is important to accept responsibility here if necessary. I am not suggesting that you take the blame. This is about owning up to your role in it if you had anything to do with it. There are many cases where one person pushes the other person to a place of emotional cheating by being verbally or emotionally abusive. The victim may not know how to process the pain, so he or she retreats, and in that space, they meet someone nice and welcoming. Not wanting to just end the relationship with the spouse, they entertain the new conversation because it's a new feeling. Before he or she realizes, this new conversation has become emotional cheating. The frequency of the conversations picks up, and eventually the spouse who caused the pain in the first place discovers the conversations. Now the verbally abusive partner has an offense to hang over the spouse's head, and the abuse gets worse. The spouse who stepped outside of the relationship seeking relief is now left to feel like a horrible person, when in fact, their spouse was just as guilty in this incident. A very important part of forgiveness is to understand if and where we were a part of the problem. If I verbally abused my wife to the point that she began to entertain the conversation of another man, I can't fault her 100 percent. I have to accept the role I played in pushing her to that point. I could blame her and hold a grudge against her for what she did to me if I want to, but it's not fair because I played a major part in it.

On the other hand, if I own up to my actions and accept the role I played, I can forgive her for her actions much easier. After we both own up to our roles, we can begin the healing and forgiving process. I would have to apologize for being verbally abusive, and she would apologize for emotionally cheating. We would look ourselves in the mirror and accept our wrong, then begin to move forward. This isn't the time to point a finger and continue to harp on who did what. It's the time to accept responsibility, forgive, heal, and move forward.

If you played no part in the offense and you were an innocent bystander doing your part in the relationship, you have to consider the offense by itself. What did your partner do? How bad was it? What level would you grade it from 1 to 10, with 10 being the absolute worse offense possible? A 1 may be having a friendly conversation with someone you don't know but who could become a problem in the relationship. A 10 could be abuse or stepping outside of the relationship and having sex with someone else. Where does the offense fall on your scale? Your scale may be totally different from the examples I shared, and that's fine. It's up to you to determine the level of the offense because you're the person who has to live with it.

This is important to identify because you need to know if it's a deal breaker or not. To me, cheating would be a deal breaker. If my wife cheats on me emotionally or physically and I feel as if I was doing everything I could to be the best man for her, I would have to get some distance immediately. There is a possibility I could return and give it another try, but it would be after a lot of conversation and prayer. Your deal breakers and standards may be different. In determining the level of offense, you have to evaluate how it makes you feel about yourself. Would you feel less about yourself if you remained in the relationship?

Would you lose some self-esteem or self-respect if you stayed? Answering those questions will help you understand how great the offense is to you. If you will never be the same and never be able to love the other person wholeheartedly again, it's a very serious offense to you. If you'd hurt for a while but eventually be able to put it behind you and love like you've never been hurt, it's more of a minor offense to you. This is the thought process you have to go through. To each his own.

I've seen many people remain in a relationship after one partner has cheated, but it's never the same. I've seen many people remain in a relationship because their standards have been lowered too much because of all the pain and suffering they've endured in their life. To some people, cheating isn't the end of the world because they have been cheated on in every relationship they've ever had. To some people, abuse isn't the end of the relationship because they've been abused before. I don't recommend staying in an unsafe relationship, but neither can I judge anyone because each person's level of pain is different. All I can do is pray for you and hope that you regain the strength to love yourself again. You have to identify your level of self-love and know if your decision is causing you to settle or forgive things that are very serious offenses.

After you have processed everything, you have to decide to forgive and stay or forgive and leave. I lean on the side of making it work, but I also understand that not every situation can be rectified. I'm a realist. I don't believe in anyone being unsafe until death.

If you forgive and decide to stay, you have to forget. To forget doesn't mean that you'll never remember it. Forgetting in this sense means that you don't continue to remind your spouse of the offense. You cannot hold a grudge. You can't bring it up every time you have a disagreement. You can't hang it over your spouse's head, ready to drop it into conversation every time you get upset. You can't make your partner a prisoner to past mistakes. To forgive and forget means you forgive them and you let him or her forget about it. Yes, in a sense, you are being the bigger person. The way your partner will prove to you that he or she is the bigger person is by apologizing, working to rebuild the trust, and never making the same mistake again. They may offend you in a different way later, and the process will have to be repeated. The mistakes will go both ways, because no one is perfect. A large part of a relationship is overlooking or forgiving offenses that aren't deal breakers. It may be annoying. It may sting. But if it's not a deal breaker, you can get over it.

It will harm your relationship if you cannot move forward from past offenses. It's a waste of life. If you are still arguing over something that was done years ago, you're wasting each other's time. My father told me a long time ago, "Son, you have to love like you've never been hurt before." That advice changed my life.

It is not easy to forgive and forget, and it may be one of the hardest things you ever do. If you happen to be on the receiving end of the forgiveness, the responsibility is on you to make up for lost time. You cannot abuse forgiveness. Forgiveness is grace. Don't ever take grace for granted. Yes, it's your spouse's place to forgive you, but it is your place to rebuild trust. Rebuilding trust may mean giving up the passwords to all your devices and being an open book. It may mean doing things differently. You may have to spend more time than usual talking with your spouse. You may have to change your routines or schedule a bit to be more accommodating and present. It may mean starting over from square one, if the offense was that bad. Do what it takes to rebuild trust.

At no time does this mean you need to be abused or mistreated in any way. Forgiveness is a gift, so it should never feel like prison. You should not have to remain a prisoner to your past or have to be fighting over the offense two years from now. Yes, the subject may still pop up a year from now if it was severe, but you have to fight for the relationship. Don't take advantage of anyone's low self-esteem or unwillingness to love themselves. If you know it's a bump in the road and you can be better, do the work to get better. Read more books. Go to relationship conferences. Hire a professional to give you an outside perspective and action steps you can take to become a better person and spouse. Don't give up on love just because you're tired or bored. Do the work. No one said it would be easy; they said it would be worth it. Don't feel like the relationship is over just because a mistake was made. Search your heart, and know that you can make this relationship work and your love can last a lifetime if you both want it to.

Here are some things to think about:

1. Have you ever been hurt in a relationship? If yes, what happened?

2. Have you been hurt in multiple relationships? If yes, did it change you for the worse?

3. How many times are you willing to forgive someone for the same offense?

4. If you hurt someone you love, would you work to win his or her heart back?

5. At what point do you think it's time to let go?

6. Do you expect more grace than you're willing to give?

7. Forgiveness is something you do for yourself as well as your spouse.

8. To forgive and forget doesn't mean you forget what happened. It means you stop reminding your spouse about it.

9. Forgiveness goes both ways. One day, you, too, will need forgiveness.

10. Don't take forgiveness for granted.

ten

LOVE LIKE GOD

And further, submit to one another out of reverence for Christ. For wives, this means submit to your husbands as to the Lord. For a husband is the head of his wife as Christ is the head of the church. He is the Savior of his body, the church. As the church submits to Christ, so you wives should submit to your husbands in everything. For husbands, this means love your wives, just as Christ loved the church. He gave up his life for her to make her holy and clean, washed by the cleansing of God's Word. He did this to present her to himself as a glorious church without a spot or wrinkle or any other blemish. Instead, she will be holy and without fault. In the same way, husbands ought to love their wives as they love their own bodies. For a man who loves his wife actually shows love for himself. No one hates his own body but feeds and cares for it, just as Christ cares for the church. And we are members of his body. As the Scriptures say, "A man leaves his father and mother and is joined to his wife, and the two are united into one." This is a great mystery, but it is an illustration of the way Christ and the church are one. So again I say, each man must love his wife as he loves himself, and the wife must respect her husband.

—EPHESIANS 5:21–33 (NEW LIVING TRANSLATION)

That is from the Holy Bible. This passage shifted everything in me when I first read it. In terms of relationships, it was the cornerstone of change for me. The first scripture says to submit to one another out of reverence for Christ. So often, we focus only on the submission of the woman, but the man is instructed to submit as well. This changed everything for me because it instructs a husband to love his wife as Christ loves the church. If you understand the sacrifice that Christ made for His church, that comparison is so great that it will take a lifetime of consistent effort. It told me that I must protect my wife's heart, mind, body, and soul. I must love myself first but then also love her as I love myself. It lets me know that if I don't love myself and respect my body, I am not fit to lead. I am not fit to marry. I am not deserving of a woman's love, trust, or submission. I must submit unto God and allow Him to change me from the inside out. Then I must love my wife with the same level of love that God has given me. I must submit unto her with love and respect. Then, in return, I will be worthy of her respect and submission in love.

In understanding this, we see that submission is a two-way street. We also see that submission isn't weakness, but it is honor, selfless love, and strength. This teaching became everything to me. There wasn't much else I had to learn about love after learning that I must love my wife with the same level of love that Christ has for me. If men learned to love their wives with that degree of love, our world would be forever changed for the better. What woman wouldn't want to love a man who loves her with that type of love?

To love like God means we must allow God to be the foundation of our relationships. God's love is pure, and pure love is the only type of love that can sustain a relationship. If love becomes toxic, it won't last.

You must share the same belief system in order for a relationship to work. Your morals and values must mirror the morals and values of your spouse. My wife and I are complete opposites in every way but our beliefs. We both believe in God. We both believe that Christ is our savior. We both believe in the teachings of the Holy Bible. That foundation determines how we love ourselves, how we love each other, how we raise our children, and how we live our lives. Our faith is our foundation, and that is what makes our relationship work. In no other way are we alike other than both liking sports. We like different foods. We enjoy different hobbies. We see everything in life from opposite perspectives, unless it's established in the Holy Bible. If anything is left up to our interpretation, we will interpret it differently. Christ is the rock. Christ is the foundation. Christ is the glue. Without the teachings of Christ, I would be a cheating man. I would be a liar, a thief, and so much more. I can't speak for who my wife would be, so you'll have to read our next book to know her side. I just know that God's love is our foundation, and it has saved our marriage.

The Good Book tells us to love our neighbors as we love ourselves. That implies that we must love ourselves first before loving anyone else. The fact that we love ourselves is what allows us to have happy and healthy relationships. Without love and respect for each other, a relationship will not work. The love, strength, and confidence needed for the relationship originate from our faith in God.

I've had personal experience with relationships where the same belief system was not shared. Without a firm foundation, a relationship can't stand. You can make it work for a period of time by your own might, but eventually you will need a power greater than yours to sustain you. I experienced that in every relationship I had until I met my wife. Obviously, they all failed until I met her. Having a like faith will call greatness out of you. Your greatness will be pulled out by your partner's greatness, and together you will strengthen each other. You will be inspired by your spouse and vice versa. The strength will be increased in both of you, and the change will be evident. Iron sharpens iron.

If the foundations are different, it will be like building a mansion on the sand. In times of storm, the relationship will sink and be destroyed. When one person is strong in his or her faith and the other is weak, most often the weaker person wins the battle. You would think that the stronger person would win, but when it comes to faith, negativity eventually becomes too big of a burden to bear. In a marriage, two become one. A double-minded person receives nothing from the Lord. It takes strong faith to achieve anything worth having. In nearly any situation, the infection spreads. One rotten apple spoils the whole bunch. An infirmity in the body will eventually affect the whole body. A negative, nonbelieving person in a marriage will eventually wear his or her spouse down.

Many years ago, my father explained it to me in very simple terms. He said, "Son, if you have on a clean white suit and you're hanging with someone who has on a dirty suit, and the two of you start to tangle up playing, who do you think will rub off on the other? Do you think your clean white will rub off on his dirty suit? Or will his dirty suit rub off on your clean white suit?" It was so simple, and I wanted to argue that it's an unfair comparison to real life, but the more I thought about it, the more I realized how simple and true it was.

I just read an email yesterday from a lady who was strong in her faith until her husband stopped attending church. She holds a position in the church and has to minister on occasion, but her husband won't attend church anymore. It upsets her, and now she feels like returning the same energy to him and not supporting him in anything he does. His energy is rubbing off on her and changing her as a person. She is stooping to his level of living and thinking, instead of requiring him to elevate to hers. In most cases, that's what happens.

In building a relationship, you have to make sure the person you're interested in dating has the same foundational beliefs as you. If you believe in Christ and His teachings but your other half doesn't, there will be many problems. You will be going in two different directions when you come to the fork in the road, and eventually you'll have to split. In difficult times, when tough decisions have to be made, it's important that the two of you be of like mind and kindred spirits. It's okay to think differently, but the basis on which you make your life's decisions must be the same. Your beliefs, morals, and values must be the same. If they aren't the same, you are simply not meant to be. There is someone for you who believes the way you do. You can be two totally different people yet stand on the same foundation.

If a woman believes that she should be loved the way Christ loves the church, but her man believes that she should be beaten when he's unhappy, their relationship will be a disaster. There are countless couples trying to make it work today with very opposing beliefs. We have gotten so caught up in physical looks that we don't bother to look within. In some cases good women are attracted to bad men and good men are attracted to bad women. The reason is that they are looking at the outer appearance instead of the heart. What does the other person believe? That's what matters most. You can't force a square peg into a round hole, even when it seems like everything else is perfect. We hope that we can change people. Rarely does that happen. If you want to take a chance, it's up to you. I've seen it happen on a few occasions, but it is very rare. The reason it's rare is that our minds resist new knowledge or change. If you meet someone in their mid-thirties, they're pretty much set in their ways and beliefs. To try to change him or her in any way will be an uphill battle where you may never reach the top. At that age people believe the way they do because their belief system has been reinforced by their life experiences. We see things for what we are, not necessarily for what they are. I could be completely wrong in my beliefs, but I doubt you'd be able to convince me of that. The same concept is true in marriage. It doesn't matter how great the sex is. It doesn't matter how many heart-to-heart conversations you have. It will be very hard to convince a person to change their foundational beliefs.

It's important to understand that foundational beliefs are not only religious beliefs. They can be beliefs about other important aspects of life. If it regards something that is important to life and your potential partner believes completely different from you, be very cautious. How can you raise children with your spouse if you believe in reasonable spanking and time-outs and your spouse does not believe in any form of chastising? How can you raise a family or live your best life if you believe in celebrating birthdays and holidays but your spouse believes all birthdays and holidays are a conspiracy of the government? How can you live your best life or raise a family if you don't believe in smoking, getting drunk, or altering the state of your mind with drugs but your partner believes marijuana is essential to life and getting drunk is a fun time? It's not just about religion, although most aspects of life can fall back on religious beliefs.

Take inventory of your beliefs, and make sure that you are building a relationship with someone with whom you can have longevity. We may all be right in our own way, but that does not mean we can make it work with just anyone. It will take a common foundation and belief system to sustain a healthy, happy relationship. I've seen thousands of couples try and thousands fail. If the beliefs are opposing beliefs, one partner will have to compromise his or her beliefs for the relationship to work. There are many interfaith couples in the world who get along just fine by the outside appearance. As I go behind the scenes as a relationship coach, I notice that one of them or both of them aren't actually practicing their beliefs. They might be of a belief or faith because they were born into it, and they still may pronounce their belief, but they do not actively live the lifestyle. Those cases cannot be counted in the argument that many interfaith couples are successful. It would be completely different if we could easily identify interfaith couples where both parties devoutly practice their separate beliefs and their relationship is truly happy and healthy. That would prove that the foundation isn't vital to the success of a relationship. With more than a decade of doing this work and studying the dynamics of healthy relationships, I have never seen that to be the case.

Many people are faced with this predicament. Do I ignore my beliefs to make this relationship work with this person who is a great person but believes totally different from me? It's a personal choice. I do not recommend it. It is one thing to have interfaith friends, family members, coworkers, and constituents. It's a totally different thing to marry and build a life with someone who has a totally different belief system. Not to venture down the path of a relationship with someone who doesn't share your faith does not mean that you hate other faiths. It means that you are not willing to compromise your foundational beliefs to try to make a relationship work. You can't feel guilty about having a belief standard. That is your right, and there is nothing wrong with standing by that right.

Here are some things to think about:

1. Do you love like God loves?

2. Have you ever been loved with God's love?

3. Have you ever tried to make a relationship work with someone of a different faith? Are you living happily ever after?

4. Would you try to make it work with someone of another faith?

5. Do you look to the Bible for instructions on love?

6. Do you believe the teachings of the Bible can sustain a relationship?

7. Your beliefs are the foundation of your life.

8. Building a relationship with someone who doesn't share your beliefs is like building a mansion on the sand.

9. You can't force anyone to change.

10. In the toughest times in a relationship, it will be your shared beliefs that carry you through.

eleven

ARGUING ISN'T COMMUNICATION

One of the most overrated experiences in relationships is arguing. I have read articles that claim arguing is actually healthy for a relationship. I guess it depends on how you define arguing. Where I come from, arguing is anything but productive. In some cases, arguing is next to life and death. I have never enjoyed the feeling of arguing, nor has my wife. I don't think it has done anything for our relationship other than tear it apart. In the first two years of marriage, we argued often, but then I decided to make some changes and that changed everything.

You go into a relationship wanting to prove yourself. There is a need to stand your ground on an issue and let your thoughts and feelings be known and heard. It's your way or the highway. There is a tug-of-war going on in a relationship every day. Who will win the battle of persuasion? Who will be the head of the household? This battle can lead to a lot of arguments and a lot of wounds that may never heal. One of the biggest lies we are told growing up is that words will never hurt us. *Sticks and stones may break my bones, but words will never hurt me.* Who made up that saying? It's one of the biggest lies we have been told. Therefore, we sling insults and demands around like we are born to do it. Words will never hurt me, right? There are arguments over everything you can imagine. Full arguments have started over who left a plate on the table. Knock-down, drag-out wars have started over who brings the most to the table. Misinformed opinions, false accusations, premature assumptions, name-calling, and screaming all make up what we call a healthy argument.

What is the difference between an argument and a disagreement? If there's no difference in your mind, that's where the problem lies. What is the difference between an argument and a discussion? If there's no difference in your mind, that's where the second problem lies. It doesn't matter what *Webster's Dictionary* has to say about the terms. What matters is how you define those things. You can have a disagreement that leads to a discussion, but it does not have to become an argument. Most couples struggle with that, they take small issues and blow them way out of proportion. When this happens it tears away at the fabric of the relationship, and it's hard to fully heal, especially when you're arguing every other day.

Arguing involves yelling, screaming, name-calling, interrupting, walking off without notice, and sometimes more. What is healthy about that? Nothing. Arguing can become addictive because of the chemicals released from the brain in a heated argument, followed sometimes with a makeup session of the ages. There is a high, a low, and then an ecstasy involved in arguments that people get addicted to experiencing. Arguing becomes a drug. First there is an assertion of power, dominance, control, or influence. Then the back-and-forth can be stimulating or arousing. The voice inflection, the passion, and the intensity stimulate the brain in a way that normal conversation does not often do. There are feelings of vindication and liberation during arguments. Some people are taking past frustrations out on the present situation. The current issue may have nothing to do with the past pain that is surfacing. Many argue about the old and the new all at once. I have met men who have admitted to having an erection while arguing. Singers have penned songs about loving arguments or when their partner is mad. There's a twisted love affair with the pain and joy of an argument. It often leads to the demise of the relationship, but couples are tricked into believing that it's beneficial.

When you argue and then make up, there's a strange feeling that comes over you. The feeling is like ointment on a wound or like a warm blanket in a cold house. The makeup session seemingly fills the void and rights all the wrongs, but rarely is that the case. It feels good in the moment, but a pattern is forming in the brain. You are teaching yourself how to argue, recover, and then prepare for the next war. In times of peace, you are preparing for war, but not to prevent it. It gets dangerous because each time you argue, your brain needs a little more intensity to get your fix. The words have to dig deeper this time. The voices need to be louder this time. There may need to be some physical contact, some furniture moving, something thrown, slammed, and the earth must shake a little. Each time you argue, it gets worse than the time before. This is why verbal assault oftentimes becomes physical assault. The same way your brain and body seemingly build a tolerance for anything ingested applies to arguing. Each time you argue, you become more desensitized to the pain of the argument. It needs to be hotter in the kitchen for you to feel the heat. Nothing satisfies the thirst for a good argument. It's toxic. It's dangerous. It's detrimental.

In coaching couples over the last decade, I've heard it all. It's actually sad to discover just how much we argue in relationships. It feels humanly impossible to not argue. It's going to happen; you just have to repackage it and learn how to have healthy disagreements. There are countless couples who argue literally every day. It's a drug. They need a hit to get high every day. I would estimate that 70 to 80 percent of couples have an unhealthy argument each week. It's just that common. They get so bad. I mean, extremely bad. You've witnessed your arguments firsthand. Well, multiply your worst argument by ten, and then you'll get a visual of what some others are going through on a regular basis. The intensity of the arguments and the stupidity for which they are started is baffling.

I don't care what you've read in the magazines. I'm reporting live from the pulse of thousands of relationships. Arguments are killing you and your relationship. It is healthy to have disagreements. It is human to disagree with another human. No two human beings will think exactly the same on every situation. It's completely normal to have a disagreement every day. As long as two humans are living together and fully functioning in their minds, there will be disagreements, and likely on a daily basis. What you have to learn is what to address and what to ignore. Not everything needs to be discussed. You have to identify if it's detrimental to the relationship. If my wife leaves something on the table or floor, that is not hurting our marriage. If she leaves the underwear of another man under the bed, that *will* affect our marriage. If my wife wants to eat at a different restaurant or can't make up her mind about what she wants to eat, that isn't going to ruin our marriage. If my wife goes out to eat with another man, that *is* going to affect our marriage. Sometimes the difference between what we should be disagreeing about and what we should ignore is drastic. You have to ask yourself and then wait for an answer before you speak on things. We are so quick with the tongue that we don't really give our brains enough time to process the situation and make an educated decision. Take your time, and don't be so quick to express your disagreements. Not everything is worth your energy. Your energy could be used in much more productive ways.

I'd like to share my communication rules that I've picked up from different experiences over the years:

1. **Wait one to twenty-four hours before addressing an issue.** This will give you time to process the situation and decide if it's worth discussing. It will also give you time to cool down. If after twenty-four hours you're still fuming, stretch it to forty-eight or seventy-two hours. It's very important that you be cool, calm, and collected when having a discussion.

2. **Have a discussion in a private setting.** It's important that you don't start a discussion in public or around other people. Things could get loud or heated, and you don't want to be around others and feel embarrassed.

3. **Use "I feel" messages.** This will help you not to point blame or label your spouse unfairly. If you use "I feel" statements, it's hard for your partner to tell you what you're not feeling. These are your feelings, and packaging them as such will help you avoid being shut down or made to feel insignificant.

4. Seek to understand and then be understood. It's much easier to solve an issue if you walk a mile in the other person's shoes. If you give him or her the courtesy of seeking to understand his or her points, hopefully he or she will do the same for you. Both parties' doing this will make it much easier to come to terms on the matter.

5. Take turns talking. Speaking in turn will help you avoid an argument. No one likes to be interrupted, and it's very rude. Practice taking turns talking.

6. Remain seated. The conversation will flow much better if both of you are seated. Standing while having a disagreement could send the wrong message through body language.

7. Do not yell. Always use the "inside voice" that you learned in kindergarten. No matter what the offense, your partner tunes you out when you start yelling.

8. Do not call names. It will do you no good to follow all the rules but still call names. If you have to call your spouse a name, make sure it's the name on his or her birth certificate.

9. Do not curse. Even though you may curse every day in normal conversation, this is not the time for it. The more you curse, the less sensitive you become to your behavior. Cursing can incite violence or reckless behavior. Keep the communication clean at all times.

10. **Listen to the other person.** Be present in the discussion. Listen to every word your spouse speaks, and hear the words. Don't move ahead or jump backwards. Be present in the conversation.

11. **Respond instead of reacting.** A response is positive, but a reaction is negative. Hear your partner, and process the meaning, intent, and feelings behind his or her words. Then respond from your heart with an open mind. Don't react out of anger or any other unproductive space.

12. **Accept responsibility for your actions.** Apologize for the role you played. Don't put an "if," "and," or "but" in your apology. Apologize from your heart without attaching an excuse to it.

13. **Keep the conversation private.** Unless the problem is something that could harm you, your spouse, or someone else, keep the conversation in-house. Your in-house business is not for the outside world to know. Yes, your parents and best friends are a part of the outside world.

14. **Take action.** It's important that you take action after the discussion. This shows growth and maturity. This is what making up is truly about. It's not about makeup sex or any of the other stuff. It's about taking action in the areas your spouse addressed.

Those are some of my communication rules. Those rules changed everything in my relationship. I learned them from experience. Then I implemented them at home. I shared them with my wife. Now we both adhere to the communication rules, and they have completely eliminated arguments. They did not eliminate disagreements, but they led to healthy discussions. Disagreements with those rules in play have brought us so much closer and made our relationship legitimately healthy. People don't believe me when I tell them we don't argue. It's foreign to most people not to have arguments. Try to keep those rules in play, and your arguments will decrease and your understanding will increase.

Arguing is not cute. Arguing is not healthy. Arguing is counterproductive, like walking on a treadmill while eating fried chicken and drinking beer. Have a real discussion and get real results.

Here are some things to think about:

1. Are you a good communicator? If not, why?

2. Is your spouse a good communicator? If not, why?

3. Do you believe communication is one of the top three most important things in a relationship? If not, why?

4. What are the most common mistakes you make when communicating with your significant other?

5. What are the most common mistakes your significant other makes when communicating with you?

6. Is bad communication a deal breaker to you? If so, why?

7. How long are you willing to work on perfecting communication in your relationship?

8. Do you already keep most of the communication rules I listed? If not, do you think implementing them will drastically change your communication style?

9. Communication to a relationship is like oxygen to life.

10. If you or your spouse isn't willing to work on your communication skills, the love is lacking in your relationship.

twelve

BE HONEST

Over the years, I have learned that one of the biggest issues in relation-ships is a lack of honesty. There are many reasons why we lie. Anyone with a heart naturally does not want to hurt someone with words. We want to be gentle, loving, and kind. For most people, that feeling is in-nate. We know what criticism feels like. We know what pain feels like. We know how shocking the truth can be. Therefore, we don't want oth-ers to feel that way. There are also people who live on the other side of the spectrum. Those individuals love sharing the harsh truth. They relish the raw effect the truth has on a person. You have to find a middle ground. The truth is necessary, but how you share it is also important.

As it relates to truth telling, what type of a person are you? Are you a people pleaser? Are you the type who had a lot of pressure put on you to be perfect growing up? There's the type of person who walks on eggshells trying not to offend anyone. He wants to be perfect in everything he does. He's seeking the approval of others with almost everything he does.

He's been critiqued in the past, and it hurts. He does not want to let his parents down. Everything he does has to be perfect, and if he makes a mistake, he wants to brush over it with perfection. He's afraid to fail because he can't bear to hear the disappointment in his mother's voice.

Then there's the person who just doesn't care who he hurts. He's brutally honest because someone was brutally honest with him. All his life he was hit with the raw truth. For years it made him cry, until eventually he learned to let it roll off his back like water off a duck. As a result, he formed a habit of telling the unadulterated truth whenever he felt like it. He didn't care who he offended or how they received it. If he felt it, he shared it. Although I have encountered this type of person in coaching, it is significantly less common.

If your spouse tells lies because he or she fears you, disappointment, or backlash, it's up to you to create a safe zone. This is where communication comes into play. It takes honest communication to let your partner know you understand that he or she is human and will make mistakes. Assure your spouse that mistakes are human and both of you will make them. Do this weekly. Open up a dialogue of vulnerable honesty until your spouse reciprocates. Express the importance of honesty and trust. Let it be known that honesty is a pillar in every successful relationship. You may have to undo the damage you may have done in the past when you would overreact to your spouse's mistakes or confessions of truth. Admit to doing it wrong. Tell your spouse that you have evaluated your past behavior and you're willing to admit that you had a habit of handling issues the wrong way. Make it known that you have changed your mind-set, read books, and gotten new knowledge that has equipped you for healthy communication. It's important to right the wrongs you've committed in the past. It won't be easy, but it is necessary. It needs to be very clear that lies are deal breakers. There must be complete honesty in the relationship for it to work and have longevity. Once trust is built or rebuilt, honesty can reside in the relationship. It is natural for someone to lie to you if they know they aren't safe around you with the truth. If there is no room for mistakes, you can expect your spouse to put up a front of perfection and live as a prisoner of your validation. There has to be room to be human.

Once you've made it clear that you've grown, changed, and created space for truth, things must change. There is no excuse for lies to be allowed in a relationship once a safe place is established. If the lies continue, there is a real issue that must be addressed. Honesty is what brings couples closer together.

What will you do with the truth when you hear it? If you reject your spouse's honesty, he or she will stop sharing with you. Creating a safe place doesn't only mean that you don't throw things, scream, yell, curse, or get physical. It also means you don't invalidate your spouse's words with your words of rebuttal. You can ruin the safe place even with quiet, room-tone responses that discredit your spouse's feelings. It's very important to be mindful of what you do in response to his or her honesty.

You have to evaluate what they are saying and then respond to it truthfully and fairly. If your spouse says he or she needs more time and attention from you, you can't make excuses about all the work you have to do and how bills are piling up. You have to accept that you've been distant and vow to prioritize better and satisfy your spouse's emotional needs. Your spouse is letting you know that he or she is okay forgoing some financial security for some emotional security. It's how they feel, and you have to respect that.

On the flip side of that, if your spouse says he or she is about to cheat unless you allow a threesome, you have a totally different problem. No matter what the truth, if it is asking you to compromise your morals or self-respect, it must be rejected. If you are against something on the grounds of ethics, morals, religion, or other bases, that is your right. It doesn't matter how your spouse feels if it goes against your self-respect or belief system. If they ask within the boundaries of marriage, you have to hear that truth.

Your spouse might express to you that he or she needs more physical intimacy. Your conversations are great, but more physical activity in the bedroom is needed. In that case, the request is within the boundaries of marriage. You then have to respond as to why there has been a decrease in physical intimacy. The truth may point to a poorly organized schedule that leaves you drained at the end of the evening. The solution may be to prioritize, plan your tomorrows today, and maintain a strict and healthy schedule. Those changes will result in increased energy and productivity. That is the truth serving its purpose at its finest.

The truth is necessary, because without it problems arise. If there is a need in the relationship and the truth is omitted, the person guilty of omission may then step outside of the marriage in a way that will be detrimental. Stepping outside of the marriage could be as simple as sharing inside business with outsiders who can't bring any solutions to the situation. It could also mean having affairs, trying to fill a void that could have been filled if the truth had been shared in the relationship. An omission of truth could be just as bad as a lie.

Tell the truth, but tell it with respect and out of love for your spouse. Stick to only what is helpful. The truth can hurt, but then it can help. No one likes to hear the truth at first because it stings. We don't like to be confronted by truth because it requires change. It forces us to look in the mirror and make adjustments to the way we do things. The ways we do things provide comfort to us. It's very uncomfortable when you're asked to change your ways. This is where you have to be truthful with yourself. If the change will make your relationship better, then do it, as long as it does not violate your values. When it's your turn to tell the truth, do it in love. Don't share the truth in a way that is intended to degrade, demean, or damage your spouse. The purpose of the truth is not to batter but to *better* your spouse. This is why the communication rules are so important. Your delivery of the truth can nullify the truth if it's delivered the wrong way. Some things you discuss will hurt no matter how you say them. If a truth will benefit the relationship in the end, tell it like it needs to be told.

The purpose of telling the truth is to prevent problems or to solve them. Never should the truth be a weapon of destruction. The goal is to bring clarity to the situation. If you really love your spouse and you want your relationship to work, you will be honest. You do more damage by holding on to something that needs to be shared. Those painful conversations can save your relationship and bring the two of you much closer together.

The presence of truth is not synonymous with the absence of discretion. You must choose what you share wisely. Letting your spouse know the woman's butt in front of you is nicer than hers is an abuse of the truth. That seems obvious, but many relationships fail because of a misuse of the truth. Although that butt may, in fact, be nicer than your spouse's, it is not beneficial to your relationship to mention it. Instead, focusing on the comparison shows you don't deeply love your spouse. Your goal is to demoralize and demean your spouse, and that has no place in love. The need to demoralize and demean is an indication that something is wrong with you on the inside and you are acting out of self-hate. Your disrespect comes from the flawed self-esteem you have within yourself, and *that* is the truth that must be addressed. The same goes for women who share unnecessary truths. Yes, another man may make more money than your man, but it does not mean your man is any less of a man. Numerous men have come to me expressing their hurt because their spouse constantly compares them to other men. The woman is being truthful about her feelings, but it's an unnecessary truth that provides no benefit to the relationship. A woman who does this is acting out of her own self-hate and bringing her man down with her because she does not want to feel like a failure alone.

Not all truth is good truth. Sometimes your truth reveals more about you than it does about your spouse. It's important to know the difference between a good truth and a bad truth. A good truth should be shared. A bad truth should be recognized and dealt with internally. If you need help with the bad truth, uncover the root and share it with someone who can help you heal from the pain.

There are some very honest conversations my wife and I have had that have propelled our marriage to higher heights. I value honesty. I value the mirror of truth and self-responsibility. It's important that as you share the truth with your spouse, you also share the truth with yourself.

Another form of truth that is not always beneficial is admission of past mistakes that have no bearing on your present relationship. Yes, you may have guilt over things you've done in the past, but if it has no effect on your spouse in the present, there is no need to uncover those things. I have coached many clients who felt the need to share with their spouse every experience they've had in the past. That is not necessary, even if your spouse asks you. Some things have no benefit of sharing. It's okay to say, "That is my business, and it has no bearing on the present." A part of being human is making mistakes and experiencing things that only God understands. A part of making mistakes is receiving grace. If you made a mistake and you were graced enough to get past it without it blowing up in your face, accept that grace. There is no need to penalize yourself when God has already granted you grace. You may need to confess to a spiritual leader. Maybe you feel that you must tell someone about the offense. You must understand that His grace is sufficient. If you have asked God to forgive you, it's forgiven. If it didn't blow up in your face, it's because you've been granted grace and you need to move forward and not repeat the error again. If the lesson has not been learned and you take the grace for granted, you will repeat the offense. Then it will blow up in your face, and that is when the truth needs to be shared about your actions because sharing the truth will help you begin the process of change.

The same goes for things that have happened to you. You have to be careful what truth you share and with whom. If you feel there is a safe place with your spouse and sharing a past experience will bring you closer, it's okay to share it. If you don't feel it will benefit the relationship in any way, nor is it hurting the relationship in any way, it does not need to be shared. People who have their heart in the right place understand and respect privacy. It should not be our desire to know every single detail about our spouse, as some things are okay to be left between that person and God. Does it matter today? Will it hurt the relationship if it's not shared? Will it help the relationship if it *is* shared? If the answer to those questions is no, move on. Keep in mind that people who are not where they need to be in life can use your truth against you in a very hurtful way. I have coached women who opened up with their spouses about painful past experiences. Those painful experiences were later thrown in their faces during an argument. Those women, who had suffered so much, were then blamed for what had happened to them as children or young adults. That is the risk when sharing your truth. It's your personal choice, so let no one make you feel guilty for not sharing every detail of your life. In such instances, an omission of truth isn't a lie, nor is it as bad as a lie. We are not instructed to trust other humans with all of our worries and pain. We are instructed to trust God. If God has it under control for you, it's perfectly okay to leave it there.

Walk in truth, and know what truth needs to be shared in your relationship. Don't sweep pressing issues under the rug. Speak up, but do so from a place of love. Relationships need an open line of communication, and we need for that communication to be honest. Trust your intuition, and do what is best for your relationship.

Here are some things to think about:

1. Have you ever lied to your significant other? If so, why?

2. Has your significant other ever lied to you? If so, did you lose all trust?

3. Will you forgive a lie? If not, why?

4. Do you feel there is ever a time to lie?

5. Do you agree with the statement "What you don't know won't hurt you"?

6. Have lies ever ended a relationship for you?

7. Can you be 100 percent truthful with your significant other?

8. You lie because you fear something. What do you fear in your relationship?

9. You don't lie to those you love.

10. Lies will hurt you before they help you!

thirteen

IS IT WORTH BREAKING UP OVER?

You have heard the advice to pick your battles wisely. It's so important in a dating relationship. It can make or break what you are trying to build. We want to make it work. We want to hold on for dear life and ride it out. No sane person enjoys breaking up and starting over with someone new over and over again. Coming to the realization that a relationship isn't going to work is painful. Even after admitting it won't work, it's not always easy to let go. We struggle with starting over. We have a hard time cutting ties and healing from the brokenness. Starting over can be a painful and tedious process, so it's very important to identify what will cause a breakup.

What are your deal breakers? How much can you tolerate? How many chances will you give? You have to know those things going into the relationship, or you'll settle for anything. Knowing your deal breakers is a part of self-love. You have to know what you will and will not tolerate. This will help you pick your battles more wisely.

No matter what the deal breaker is, there are precursors. Identify the small things that can eventually lead to the big things. Cheating may be a deal breaker for you. But what leads to cheating? What do you consider to be cheating? Is flirting in the Facebook message inbox considered a form of cheating? Could flirting in the Facebook message inbox lead to a physical affair? Is emotional cheating a serious offense in your book? What about your girlfriend going out to lunch with someone whom she could be attracted to? Think about all the different scenarios that could arise, and decide on your response to them. If the act is a precursor of something bigger, it needs to be addressed. That small thing could lead to a big thing. That is an issue worth addressing.

Is lying a deal breaker for you? If so, does that apply only to big lies, or do little lies count in the same way? What is a little lie? What is a big lie? If your boyfriend withdraws money from your account at the ATM, loans it to a friend, but lies to you when you ask about the purpose of the transaction, is that a big or a little lie? Is that something that could lead to the end of the relationship? If so, it needs to be addressed and established as a deal breaker.

It's very important to know what your deal breakers are, because that will determine what issues you should address and what issues you can ignore. If you don't know what a deal breaker is, that is your first order of business. For some men, a woman who doesn't cook daily is a deal breaker. That isn't a deal breaker for me. For some men, a wife who doesn't have sex on demand is a deal breaker. That isn't a deal breaker for me. I'm concerned mostly with the matters of the heart. Can I trust my wife while I'm away for work? Can I trust that I'm not sleeping next to the enemy? On the other hand, my wife has to trust me while I am out of town. She has to trust me when I am coaching different women around the world. Trust is a key part of the foundation of a relationship. Remove the trust, and you lose everything. Where do your concerns lie? What are you most worried about in your relationship?

I've seen and heard it all. I have heard some very petty stories regarding relationships. I once heard of a physical fight breaking out in a relationship because the guy held the door open for another woman at the grocery store. Somehow that small act led to a sly comment, then a sly rebuttal, and the rest is history. Before you know it, there's yelling and cursing and she's throwing punches. Something is very wrong with that picture. Some couples argue every day. Some couples argue multiple times a day. That's because the deal breakers have not been established.

In my household, I created a rule that states, "If it's not worth breaking up over, it's not worth arguing over." That doesn't mean we don't discuss smaller issues. It means we don't dwell on small issues, nor do we argue over them. The undoing of many relationships is the act of picking the wrong battles. In a relationship, battling is very draining. It wears you down and chips away at the foundation of your relationship. After a period of time, you become very battle-weary. Your judgment weakens when you're weary. One thing leads to another, and the smallest of issues can completely ruin a relationship, all because the wrong battle was chosen. It can't be an all-or-nothing type of deal. You don't have to address every issue, nor should you ignore every issue. You have to be wise enough to pick and choose the things that could potentially lead to a breakup and discuss them.

The whole goal of this lesson is to get your relationship beyond the point of petty. Don't be a Petty Betty, arguing just because it gives you purpose in life. Fighting with your boyfriend should do nothing for you other than drain you.

There is a technique in behavioral science that teaches you to ignore, redirect, and reinforce. My wife and I learned this while working in the group home system. We were dating at the time and got married shortly after that. We brought that knowledge home and began using it in our relationship. It works like a charm. I was known to get "in my feelings" and catch little attitudes. My wife started ignoring my little mood swings and would move on to the next order of business, like preparing dinner. I would curl my lip a little more, and still she would ignore my attention-seeking behavior and continue forward with discussing her day or our son's day. After not getting the attention I was seeking, I was forced to shift my focus to the conversation she had initiated. She would then reinforce that behavior by conversing more and giving me more attention or affection. It was only at the point of my getting over my little attitude that she would rub my head, give me a hug, or give me some other type of physical touch. She was very purposeful in her efforts because if she had reinforced my attitude, I would have copped an attitude every time I wanted some extra attention. Remember, any behavior that is recognized and rewarded will repeat itself.

The key here is not to reinforce the wrong things. My wife purposefully ignored my mood and then reinforced my positive interactions. In turn, it taught me to stop catching attitudes for attention and instead have healthy conversation to gain attention. Ironically, although it worked like a charm on me, it also worked like a charm on her. As humans, we get moody at times for no good reason. We can walk in the door the wrong way or wake up on the wrong side of the bed. Once we're in that space, the smallest action by our spouse can set us off. If it's ignored, we are likely to get over it and get on with life. It's no different from when our firstborn had his first tantrum in the store. He fell to the ground to cry, and my wife simply stepped over him and kept walking. As soon as she stepped over him, he stopped crying and realized he was being left behind. He got up and ran to catch up. The tantrum was over. She then reinforced the good behavior and let him know that a tantrum is unacceptable. My son never threw another temper tantrum again. It may not be that easy with your child or with your spouse, but it's worth paying attention to what you're reinforcing in your relationship.

What happens so often is that one person gets an attitude, and then his or her spouse dives in and gives him or her attention for it. This attention is oftentimes negative attention. Then this very small thing becomes a big argument. Instead, if there is something bothering you, assess whether or not it is worth the time and energy to deal with it, and if it is, speak on it. If it's trivial, let it go and move on. It's hard to get beyond the insignificant conflicts and drama, but it is rewarding when you do. In the beginning, you may just have to be quiet for a few minutes and coach yourself. Repeat to yourself, "Don't be petty, don't be petty, get over it, let it go." Recite and repeat whatever it is you need to say to yourself to get you past the petty.

We spend too much time focusing on the wrong things, and that's what costs us our relationships. In order to have a long, healthy relationship, you must choose your battles wisely. Evaluate why you like to focus on insignificant issues. Is it for control? Is it for attention? Is it a habit you picked up in your last relationship? Is it what you saw your parents do? Is it behavior you picked up from your friend's relationship? Evaluate your pettiness, and keep it in check.

I have seen many people lose a relationship because the arguments drained their partner so much that it had to end. You may be wired for drama, but others may prefer to save the drama for the movies. Drama and pettiness are not cute, and they hurt your relationship in the long run.

If it's not worth breaking up over, it's not worth arguing over. Focus on what matters, and ignore what does not. Use your energy to better your relationship instead of tearing it down. Don't push away a good person because you want to nitpick over little things that serve no purpose in the big picture. Don't waste your time or the time of your spouse. There are many major issues that will arise, and you will appreciate having reserved your energy for issues that really matter. A relationship is a marathon, not a sprint. If it was a sprint, you could afford spending the energy to argue about every little thing, but you have a long journey ahead of you, so use your energy wisely.

This may take some relearning. It's perfectly fine to change your ways and become a better person. Just because you're accustomed to toxic relationships that dwell in the shallow end, it doesn't mean you have to stay there. Look at those relationships and the outcome of them. Pay attention to what happens to people who are stuck in relationships built on weak foundations. Good people who love themselves will not tolerate a messy situation for long. You will lose the one you love if you don't focus your energy in the right areas. Some things to focus on are healthy communication, loving affection, quality time, and kind words. Don't major in minor things.

Here are some things to think about:

1. Have you ever ended a relationship over something very petty?

2. Do you regret having let a relationship go?

3. Have you ever had to take a break in a relationship because a small issue became a big issue?

4. Have you identified your deal breakers?

5. Have you ever been with someone who had unfair deal breakers?

6. Know what's important and what isn't.

7. Have a clear understanding of what your spouse's deal breakers are.

8. Trust your intuition.

9. Don't focus on the petty.

10. A deal breaker can be forgiven but not taken for granted.

fourteen

PICK A CAPTAIN

It takes humility to admit your weaknesses. Most people believe they are strong in areas where really they need work. It's natural to be a know-it-all in your own right. Your way always seems to make the most sense from your perspective. At times you may be right. But consider that you may be right just because you can see it only through your own lenses. It's not easy admitting that someone is stronger than you in certain areas. Telling your partner that he or she is smarter than you might not be the easiest thing you do in your relationship.

A captain is needed in all areas of your life. Your brain is the captain of your body. Companies have chief executive officers, owners, presidents, vice presidents, and so on. Some companies have a captain for each of the different departments. People are given the room to be the best in their area of expertise. Authority is delegated, and things run better that way because many minds working in concert are always better than one. If one person is in charge of every aspect of the business, its success will be limited. Different minds operate differently, and there is strength in our differences.

Captains are needed for structure and order. There has to be a head in everything we do, or else there will be chaos. Although this looks different in a healthy relationship, it is still a fact. The captain is the leader, but a good leader is not a dictator. Even though you may be the head in your area, that does not mean you don't seek the counsel of others. You have the final say-so, but that doesn't mean you know it all.

A classroom has a teacher. The country has a president. A football team has a head coach. In life, most operations run on a hierarchy. Imagine never being able to make a decision about anything in your household because no one wants to step up and lead in that area. That would be absolutely miserable. At some point, someone has to confirm the decision and then take action.

How does this look in a healthy relationship? Contrary to common belief, this is not a dictatorship. The man is not the know-it-all, and neither is the woman. There should not be one person wearing the pants in the relationship. Wearing the pants does not mean that's who is leading. It could be a skirt or a dress leading. The lead is not an overall position. You lead where you're strong and follow where you're weak.

In my household, my wife gives me the final say-so in a lot of areas, but she has the final say-so in just as many, if not more. I once thought that for the man to be the head of the household, he had to run everything. But even the president of a country has advisers. Kings have advisers. So being the head does not mean the man knows everything and can make healthy decisions for the family in every area. Many people believe that leadership is dictatorship and that role belongs to the man. That's very unhealthy, because that level of power can create a monster.

A man who is unchecked in his relationship can destroy his family from the inside out. It's important that, as adults, we identify our strengths and weaknesses and we relish our roles.

My wife is in charge of deciding on schoolwork and education for the children. I would gladly send our sons to public school because it would save us around $30,000 a year. But she feels the education and the environment are very important for our boys, so she chose to put them into private school. I'll share an interesting fact with you. She put them into private school way before we could afford it. We were using financial aid and paying less than most parents spend in day care each month. Most parents don't even try to send their kids to private schools because they automatically assume it's too expensive and figure there's no way financial aid can reduce the payments to where they can afford them. That's not true. My wife stepped out on faith, and even though we didn't have much money, she got our son into a reputable school. Over the years, our businesses grew and we were able to pay the full tuition without relying on financial aid. I cringe every month when the school tuition hits our account, but I conceded that authority to her because she understands those things better than me. She gives me the say-so over financial decisions, although she executes them. She trusts that I will make the right financial decisions for our family because I'm hands-on with our income. She has control over the house, decorating, and all parties and events. I could be a tyrant and make a fuss about those things just because I'm helping to pay for them, but I know it's not my strength.

There are so many decisions that have to be made in a relationship, family, and household. There are endless opportunities to show humility in yourself and confidence in your spouse. You have to know your strengths and weaknesses and be content operating in your areas of expertise. Even in the areas where you are the head, you should consult your spouse before making a final decision. They may have some input that broadens your perspective and helps you make the most appropriate decision. Any decision made will affect everyone else in the family, so be mindful of that.

Occasionally, switching roles can give both partners a greater understanding of what the other person has to go through in his or her position. It will help you gain understanding and appreciation for the role they play in the relationship. A relationship should feel equal. It should not feel like a warden and a prisoner, a boss and a worker, or a master and a slave. It should feel like teamwork, not dictatorship. You may have an urge to express your every thought and feeling and try to dominate every situation, but you have to trust your spouse. Allow mistakes to be made, and then learn from them. I have made some really stupid mistakes over the years, and so has my wife. We have a little chuckle at each other when a mistake is made, but it's all love.

At some point, if you discover that the wrong person was put in charge of a particular area, make modifications and try something new. I have coached couples who struggle in certain areas because the person in charge should not have been in charge. Couples have come home to find their electricity disconnected because the person in charge of paying the bills forgot to pay them. That's a sign that something needs to be addressed and reassigned. I have coached couples who lost thousands of dollars because the one in charge of their business investments didn't know what he or she was doing and squandered money on bad investments. That has to be discussed, and changes have to be made without pride and dignity getting in the way.

There are traditional roles that have been put into place, but that may not work for your family. In some relationships, the man cooks dinner and washes the dishes. Traditionally, the woman fulfilled that job. In many cases, the traditional roles do not fit. A lot of top chefs are men. So why is it we expect the woman to do all the cooking? You have to pay attention to the roles in your household and make sure they fit. My wife remembers to take out the trash more often than I do, but taking out the trash is typically the man's job. For many years I did the school drop-off and took our kids to sports practice, but that is traditionally seen as the woman's role in the minivan. That may still be the case for many families, but if it does not work for your family, don't force it to be that way.

Pick a captain in each area, and respect the order. Collaborate and communicate, but respect each other's strengths and weaknesses. Don't get trapped in traditional roles if those roles don't work for your household. A relationship is about submitting to each other. That means the man will lead in some areas and the woman will lead in others. There should not be an alpha male running every aspect of the household, just as there shouldn't be an alpha female running every aspect. If one spouse is dictating and dominating in every area, that means the other is suppressed and not using his or her gifts. That weakens the relationship, and eventually it will fall apart. No one should have to silence his or her voice or live on his or her knees. It takes two to make it work, and both sexes were given the tools to help build a healthy, long-lasting relationship.

Here are some things to think about:

1. Do you know your role in a relationship?

2. Have you ever been a dictator in a relationship?

3. Have you ever been suppressed in a relationship?

4. Do you fit the roles that are traditionally given to you?

5. Are you open to doing the opposite of tradition to make your relationship work?

6. Be humble in yourself and confident in your spouse.

7. Know your strengths and weaknesses.

8. Traditional roles might not be right for your family.

9. Relish your role!

10. Every team needs a captain!

fifteen

BE TEAMMATES

You would think this is common sense, but I have come to find out that it's not. So many of us compete against our spouses. I have been guilty of it. There are many ways to compete against your spouse. You may be totally unaware that you are doing it.

If you have ever competed against your spouse in an unhealthy way, the issue lies within you. I'm not talking about your weight loss competition or savings competition. Have you ever belittled your spouse? Have you ever lied to your spouse? Have you ever manipulated your spouse? Have you ever deceived your spouse? Have you ever taken advantage of your spouse? Have you ever been jealous of your spouse? Have you ever lied about or even stretched the truth about your spouse? If so, you've treated him or her like an opponent. It makes absolutely no sense to be opponents in the same household, yet we do it. As people, we are competitive by nature. We love to compete and keep up with others. Our lives are built around keeping up with our neighbors. If we did what we wanted to do the way we know we are supposed to do it, no one would be in debt. We would live in a totally different world if we didn't want to compete and beat our opponents in everything we do. It wouldn't be perfect, but it would for sure be different.

Of course in some cases, competition is great. There is a healthy way to compete in a relationship. Compete to show the most love. Compete to do the most chores. Compete to be the most affectionate. Compete to get the fittest. Those are competitions worth doing. We don't often do that though. Usually in those cases, one person is giving his or her all and the other person is just receiving it all. Some people are just takers by nature. Some people are lazy, greedy, selfish, and all the other things that go with taking. It could be their upbringing. It could be their culture. It could be their mind-set. There could be a million and one reasons why they are that way.

I have seen both men and women give, give, and give to their spouses and receive very little in return. If you are with a taker, it's an unhealthy situation. There are good teammates, and there are bad teammates. I was able to see this up close and personal when I became the life coach for NBA and NCAA teams. It was interesting to see the different personalities on a team. I played sports all my life and even in college, but I never noticed it the way I did as an outsider. The good teammate shows up to practice with a smile and great energy. He talks, laughs, and jokes with his teammates in a genuine way. He practices hard and then stays after to do a little more training. On game nights, he gives his all and he supports his teammates. It's not all about him. He wants all his teammates to look good in their respective positions because it helps the team as a whole. If he's on the bench, he's vocally supporting those in the game. He's as happy for their success as he is for his own. He doesn't allow anyone to run over him or take advantage of him. He's fun and fair. He's very rare because these attributes just do not come easy.

On the other hand, I have seen the bad teammate. He's divisive. He lies. He manipulates. He uses. He's jealous, self-centered, and very selfish. He goes hard when it's in his best interest, and he pouts when the spotlight isn't on him. Then, when things get out of hand, he blames everyone around him and accepts no responsibility for his actions. He's the worst type of teammate you can have.

Now take those two personalities and put them into a relationship. It's very obvious who would be better in a relationship. Naturally, the bad teammate is usually horrible in relationships outside of the sport, too. I've noticed that bad teammates usually aren't married before thirty-five years of age. They fire people and switch teams all the time. They project all their problems onto others, and nothing seems to go right for long. If you're a bad teammate, the same things happen in a relationship.

In a relationship, you have to be teammates, not opponents. I once posted a quote about this concept, and it received nearly 1 million shares on Facebook. That proved to me how important this lesson is, but also how rare it is. If you truly love someone, it shouldn't be hard to be happy for his or her wins in life. The other person's wins are your wins too. You're a couple; you're one.

The obvious side of being a teammate is to be loving and supportive. It's not easy for everyone, but it has to be learned at some point. You have to be happy to see your spouse get a promotion, even if your own promotion has not come yet. You have to be happy to see your spouse living his or her dreams, even when your own dreams are temporarily a nightmare. It's important that you breathe life into your spouse. Be positive, encouraging, and uplifting. Go above and beyond to support your spouse in his or her business and ventures. Buy something that will help him or her in that area of their life. Surprise him or her with more love and support. It's most important to be supportive when things are not going your way. It won't be easy, but if you can teach yourself to do it, your relationship will be better for it.

Another important aspect of being a teammate is wanting to see your spouse have a life outside of you. Encourage your spouse to have a night out with friends for some clean fun. It does not mean you have to support things that will push him or her further away from you, cause them to lust, fall into sin, or get into trouble. Going to a game, seeing a play, or going out to eat are outings you can support to show you want your teammate to enjoy a social life. Support your partner's life outside of you because it's healthy and needed at times. If it's too often, like multiple times a week, address the frequency with concern and respect. If it's healthy activity and you know you can trust your spouse, support it.

Do not attempt to hinder your spouse's relationship with his or her family; encourage it! There are times that family can be toxic and the interactions cause a lot of pain. Address those issues, and get to the bottom of them. But if the communication and interaction are healthy, support them. I have coached people who had to distance themselves from their parents or siblings because the relationships were so toxic. That's understandable, but if the relationship is not toxic, you should be comfortable with your spouse being close to his or her family. It's a sign of control and abuse if you isolate your spouse from loving friends and family, even if he or she is willing to abide by your rules.

Your spouse is not an opponent you should try to dominate and control. You are teammates who should strive to win together instead of defeating each other. It's surprising to see how many people are sleeping with the enemy. The number of couples I coach in this situation is alarming. We have to fix that. We have to learn to work together, win together, grow together, and live together in peace and happiness.

We know we should be supportive and loving, but it also goes deeper than that. Being a teammate means being true friends. It means being honest. It also means operating with integrity and loyalty. You can convince your mouth to say that your spouse is your teammate, but if your actions don't back it up, you're lying. If you're belittling your spouse, you are not teammates. If you get upset and use words to attack, you are opponents. Think about the words you use in your relationship. Are those words edifying or demoralizing? Maybe you thought you were teammates, but if you're tearing your spouse down with every argument you have, that's not being a team. The words you use to tear your spouse down may leave lasting damage. Those words can destroy any self-esteem left from childhood. Words have a lot of power, and they can do a lot of good or a lot of harm. When speaking to a teammate, you should motivate and encourage, not criticize and demoralize. I get it, though; you speak from your heart, and if you're hurting, your words will tend to hurt others. Think about your words, and ask yourself if you are helping or hurting.

As teammates, you must be honest with each other. Are you a little liar or a big liar? Little lies eventually have a big impact on the relationship. Are you lying big or small? It doesn't really matter. If you're lying to your spouse, you are not teammates. How can a team win if the members of that team are not honest with one another? It takes honest communication to get on the same page and remain there. If you're lying every other day, you will never truly be in sync with your spouse, and eventually that will cost you the relationship. Honesty needs to be across the board in relevant matters. How you kissed in your past is not relevant to the present. What you are doing and who you are doing it with today are what matters. You cannot lie about the communication or interaction you're having with others. You cannot lie about the decisions you're making. You cannot lie about how you spend your money or your time. To be teammates means you are open and honest. Honesty is essential to building a strong team poised for success. Many couples grow accustomed to lying to save face or deceive their spouse. It's dangerous, and it works against everything you say you stand for in a relationship.

Another major part of being teammates is being faithful in every area. One of the main ways couples work against each other as opponents is by cheating. It does not matter if the cheating is emotional or physical; either way, it's still cheating. If you can't be faithful to your spouse, it means your spouse is your enemy and you don't truly love your spouse the way you should.

Truly think about the concept of being teammates and not opponents. This will change the way you look at a lot of things in your relationship. Take it outside the context of a relationship, and think about an actual team you've played on or been a part of in another capacity. Make your own list of attributes you feel a team needs to be successful. So often, we treat others better than we treat our partners. If you think about the behavior on an actual team, it will help you clearly see how you may be cutting corners in your relationship that you wouldn't cut on your team at work.

Admit to the areas you need to work on, and help your spouse identify the things he or she should improve, too. Then help each other develop and get stronger in those areas. Be loving, supporting, under-standing, compassionate, and forgiving. Work together as a team train-ing to win the Championship of Love. If you wouldn't cheat yourself in an actual game, why cheat yourself in your relationship? You may be able to make subtle changes without it being too obvious to your part-ner that you weren't being a great teammate in the past. Sometimes we just need to make little tweaks to be better. You may be doing the wrong things and know it, but it hasn't surfaced in your relationship yet. If you still have time to get ahead of the issues that could one day arise, do so. Don't hurt yourself by trying to get over on the person on your team. You are in this thing together, not against each other. Make it work by doing it the right way!

Here are some things to think about:

1. Are you teammates or opponents?

2. Have you ever been with an opponent in a relationship? If so, how long did it last?

3. Why do you think we compete in relationships?

4. If you've been an opponent with your spouse, what will you do to change?

5. If your spouse has treated you like an opponent but wants to change, will you forgive?

6. What does it mean to you to be a teammate with your spouse?

7. What does your dream team look like?

8. If you treat each other like teammates instead of like opponents, you will win at life!

9. There is no "I" in "team."

10. Cheating and lying are treating your spouse like an opponent.

sixteen

LEADING IN LOVE

For many couples, the man is the head of the household. In some cases, that's toxic because the man is a tyrant. In other cases, the man is designated the head just to stroke his ego because he doesn't actually run anything; his wife just lets him think he does. It may seem that men have power but women have influence. The man may be the head of the household, but if the woman influences all his decisions, it makes her the leader. Even the children have different relationships with Mommy and Daddy. Mommy is the nurturer and caretaker. She can be a disciplinarian, too, but more chances are taken with her. If Daddy is the disciplinarian, it's usually a bit more intimidating and he's taken more seriously when he's upset. On the other hand, Daddy can be putty in his daughter's hands. It's a give-and-take. There is always some type of order in every household, even if it's out of order.

Men love to be in charge. Men love to feel in charge. Men love to lead. Men want to be revered and respected. I don't know why it's that way, but it is. That is why I want to speak to the men in this chapter! It's very important that we look at our roles from every angle to better understand how we should operate in our homes as head of the household.

We lead because we believe we were intended to lead and instructed to lead. Adam was created first and given dominion over the earth, and we believe we are his descendants. Eve exerted a woman's influence very early on, and that shifted the world in a way beyond our understanding. A man was placed in power but a woman was given so much influence. Why didn't the serpent tempt Adam? The serpent knew who really had the influence. It knew who thought with both sides of the brain and would be able to rationalize the new information and see greater possibilities than the current ones. It was up to Adam to make the final call and remain obedient. Would Eve have put him in a headlock and choked him out if he had refused to bite the apple? As you can see, the head of the household isn't a dictator. He's entrusted with the responsibility of making the right call for his family. Adam could have reminded Eve of the law and declined, but he didn't. Everything happens for a reason. The same dynamic is common in many relationships today. Many men don't know how to say no to their wives because we've been taught that a happy wife makes for a happy life. There is a lot that goes into that.

A man is given free rein to lead and to live as he pleases. He can choose his destiny with his daily actions. A man can lead a household to peace and prosperity through his actions and obedience to God. Although women are very influential, they will listen to a strong and loving man any day of the week. As men, we have gone wrong and fallen short in most cases regarding leadership. We equate leadership with dictatorship, and that begins the breakdown of our homes. If you feel the need to control every situation, it means you fear something. If there is trust, there will be no need for control. You can care and show concern without controlling. Leadership is actually service. You have to serve your family as the head of the household. You serve with love.

Many men cut off the head of the woman and live with only her body. This type of man does not allow his wife to think. He does everything and runs everything, so the wife is like a helpless deer standing and staring into the headlights of the car that is about to demolish her. As a leader, a man should encourage his wife to reason and utilize her intelligence. He should urge her to be who God has called her to be. She has a special set of skills that cannot be replaced or duplicated. She thinks with both sides of her brain, while he thinks with only one side of his. Her life expectancy is longer. Her tolerance level is higher. She is wonderfully and magnificently designed. A true leader will see the potential in that and encourage her to flourish in her unique abilities. The man's job is to lead objectively and to remain unbiased and aware. A man views things differently than a woman does; that difference should be a benefit, not a hindrance. The two must work together.

Leading in love means the man should set the standard for the type of love that will sustain the relationship. So often, as men, we want to receive first. We want a girlfriend to treat us like a husband. We want a woman to lie down with us before we give her a lifetime commitment. We want her to have our children but not have peace of mind that we are in the trenches with her for the long haul. So often we put the cart before the horse. In a lot of ways, we lead backwards and then wonder why things fall apart. As men, we have to lead in love. There is strength in gentleness. We don't have to dominate or dictate. We just have to love.

Being born a leader doesn't mean you know how to lead. It means the world has put you into a position, but that doesn't mean you are qualified to fill it. Think about leadership and what it takes to lead. Who can lead you? How does that person lead? Do you like your leader? Do you love your leader? Do you respect your leader? What is his or her leadership style?

God is my leader. I've studied His leadership style and taken notes. He leads by example. His word gives me examples of how I should carry myself as a Christian. He is gracious. He is merciful. He is compassionate. He understands. He is forgiving. He loves. That is leadership. Evaluate your leadership, and ask yourself if you lead in those same ways. Do you have God-like qualities in your leadership? Why do you follow God? I follow Him because there is balance. There is peace. There is instruction but also free will, compassion, and forgiveness. The instruction is given in love. The free will means I can do anything I set out to do. I'm not under a dictatorship. The compassion means He forgives me when I stumble. The love is forgiving, and it renews every day. Whether you believe in God or not, His methodology is an amazing model for love and leadership.

How can you say you follow God if you don't lead like Him? How can your woman trust you if you say you're a man of God but your love doesn't feel like God's love? Ephesians 5 highlights this; leading in love means you give the love you'd like to receive. Speak to your wife with respect. Speak to her with compassion and love. There is no need to raise your voice, curse, or demean her. There is no need to berate her. Speak to her the way you would want a leader to speak to you.

Treat her. Take care of her mind. Speak life into her soul. Encourage her to pursue her dreams and use every gift she possesses. Then put your money where your mouth is, and invest in her gifts. Give her tips and ideas from your wonderful business mind, and support her every step of the way.

Hold deep conversations with her. Talk about everything under the sun and what makes the world go round. Make love to her mind, not just her body. Treat her mind like a treasure and explore it. Get to know her in every way. Enjoy her conversation no matter how trivial it may seem. If she's speaking about something, it's important to her. Make her likes your likes, and respect the differences between the two of you.

Take care of her body. Hold her heart with care. Hold her hand in public. Run your fingers through her hair, long or short. Caress her body every chance you get. Fall in love with every inch of her waist and love her from head to toe. Even the Bible tells you to ravish in her bosom. Make her body the only body in the world.

Wash her with love. Ephesians 5 tells you that Christ presented the church blemish and spot-free. Wash your woman with love. Speak to her in a loving way that she will understand and that resonates within her. Let it vibrate to her core. She can feel you even when she can't hear you. She knows the intent behind your love, so let it be pure. Take care of her, and treat her with respect. Make her a new queen, and give her the honor that many queens of the past were not given. This is her castle, and you are her king. Operate in honor and integrity.

A leader is a servant. Don't be afraid to serve. Wash the dishes when you can. Do the laundry if she will let you. Massage her back. Rub her feet. Run her errands. Surprise her by occasionally doing for her what she can do for herself. Let her know you love and appreciate her.

Anyone can be great, because anyone can serve. The greatest among us is the servant. Those are the words of Jesus Christ, and they ring true even today. Don't just serve the world. Serve in your home. What good does it do to serve everyone outside of your home and neglect those in your home? Charity begins at home.

If there are children watching, your leadership has even more impact. Lead in a way that provides a blueprint for your children. Your son should know how to lead based on your example. Your daughter should know what a real man looks like by your example. If they do not know, you are failing them. Don't fail them any longer. Make a choice to lead in love. You are teaching your children what love is and what it looks like. Don't lie on love. Don't set your children up for failure because you refuse to lead in love. They will grow up to be your crown and glory. Don't fail them by failing to lead the right way.

Leading in love also includes standing your ground and making the decisions you know are right for your family. To lead this way does not mean you are weak or that you are a pushover. You cannot decide from any other place but love. Let true love be the guiding light. Leading in love means saying no at times. Leading in love won't always be the way your family wants to go. They may not like every decision God has asked you to make. It will make sense to them one day if you know you're doing the right thing. Don't confuse a servant leader for a weak person. Being a servant means you are strong and great, not weak. Even in service, there comes a time when saying no is appropriate. Know when you have to go against the majority and do what is right for your family. A lot of men confuse this type of leadership with lying down and being run over. That is not true. This type of leadership requires great strength, wisdom, clarity, and poise. It takes a great leader to lead in love. Anyone can be a tyrant and a dictator. It takes a special leader to lead with love.

It is my hope that your leadership will set the standard for your household. I hope your love will be seen, respected, appreciated, and reciprocated. If you chose the right woman, you should receive the same level of love in return. In most cases, if a woman is treated right, she will reciprocate with an even greater love. She was created to love. Love is in her DNA. Whereas men must learn to love, she was born to love. She's a nurturer by nature. If you ignite the love that's already within her, you may be in for the ride of a lifetime. If you suppress the love that is within her, your life will grow to be miserable. Make sure you are leading in such a way that will inspire her to love you the way God intended.

We must stop dictating and truly start leading our homes. We must give the love we wish to receive and then continue giving. We must raise the bar higher to be different from the men we saw before us. Even if you were raised around great men, there is room to be even better.

I have seen how this type of leadership affects the love between couples. I've lived through this change and seen it play out over and over again. A relationship will go only as far as the man is willing to go. If the man is unwilling to grow, the relationship is doomed from the start. It's up to the man to take the lead and provide an example. In this type of leadership style, the communication gets better and the loving gestures increase. That makes a woman feel loved and respected. It makes her feel protected. She gains confidence in her man, and she trusts they can last a lifetime together and everything will be all right. Because she isn't being mistreated, she's able to learn and grow as a person. She builds the confidence that lets her know she will be fine even if she outlives her husband, because of the knowledge he gave her and the way he supported her growth in her personal life. She isn't made to feel stupid or incapable. She is empowered and uplifted. She knows she can stand on her own, but she's content being carried at times. She is so strong and confident from this love; she knows that she could carry her man for a season if life ever asked that of her. It's all love. There's no manipulation or deception. There's no control or abuse. It's all love, and this is the type of love that will make you come alive. It lasts a lifetime, and you will want to pass it down to your children. Pure love is the greatest love, and it feels so amazing. It will literally rejuvenate you and make you feel younger. It will help you live longer and live more peacefully along the journey through life.

Rewire your mind if that is what it takes. Erase the bad and replace it with the good. Teach yourself how to lead in love. Allow yourself to shed your old ways and develop new ways. If you have been a dictator all your life, the transition may be painful. You may initially feel weak, but trust that strength is on the way. You will soon understand what it means to have strength in gentleness. There are peace and calm in healthy love. This type of love has more power and influence than dictatorship. By being loving and gentle yet strong, you will be able to influence your wife and children to elevate themselves in every way. No one likes a bully or a tough guy. What woman doesn't like a gentle, strong, confident man? I think I'd be hard pressed to find a woman who does not appreciate a man who loves her wholeheartedly the same way God loves us. This type of love can activate every ounce of love in a woman and change everything in the relationship for the better.

True love has never hurt anyone. There is nothing to lose by loving a woman the way you should. Even if you lose her, you will have gained many life lessons that will prepare you and sustain you. There is only an upside to love. It can only get better with genuine love. Make it your mission to love like never before. There will be naysayers who try to convince you otherwise. Take my word on it, I have been through it and made the transformation from dictator to lover. It's a wonderful journey to be on, and it will transform your relationship. Contrary to popular belief, it doesn't set you up to be run over. It liberates you and rewards you with the love of a lifetime. It enhances your life and makes you wish you had known sooner how to truly love.

This is real, and it can be real for you. Don't let history or family tradition keep you from real love. Don't let the backwards mind-set of society keep you from real love. Decide for yourself and your household what love will look like, and then live it out. Lead in love.

Here are some things to remember:

1. What does it mean to you to lead with love?

2. Do you feel you can make the change if you haven't already?

3. If you've made the change, did it change your woman?

4. If you lead in love and it's not appreciated and reciprocated, how will you handle it?

5. Do you believe kids can learn how to love from your example?

6. Are you afraid to be seen as weak?

7. Did you see your father or another man lead in love? If so, what did you learn from it?

8. Leading and loving are your calling in the home.

9. Love is gentle.

10. If you lead with love, your woman will reciprocate.

seventeen

SUBMISSION TAKES STRENGTH

Married women, don't put the book down. Don't set it on fire. Don't feel attacked. Don't feel belittled. Submission is not what you think it is. Yes, in biblical days, women had absolutely no rights. But even then men were instructed to be faithful, not to divorce, and to love their wives as Christ loves the church. Today, circumstances have changed so much. It is a totally new world. Things are not where they need to be, but hopefully we are making progress. Many women are still suffering in relationships. There is a lot of inequality. But the gap is closing.

It's important to understand the concept of submission as it relates to relationships. One of the greatest developments in this teaching is that husbands and wives must submit *to each other*. This is actually stated in the Bible, but somehow many Christian preachers miss that sentence. Submission takes strength. Submission takes humility. Never let your submission come from a place of fear or weakness. It should be a healthy, conscious choice.

The proper interpretation of *submission* should be to follow the lead of your husband if he is following the lead of God. It should not mean you are a sex slave. It should not mean you are like a child to your husband and he can treat you as such. It should not mean you have no voice, feelings, thoughts, or opinions. It should not mean you have to compromise your morals and values. It should not mean you are less than him. It means you are honoring God's word and allowing him to lead the household. It means that if you submit an idea and, after thorough conversation, he doesn't feel it's the way to go, you trust him, respect him, and follow his lead. If you can't do that, consider why you married him. The point of marriage is to join with someone you can love, trust, and respect. When you present an idea and your husband agrees with you and says, "Let's do it," he's actually submitting to you. Don't discount your influence. Don't feel that you're insignificant and your relationship is like slavery. If you feel like a slave in your relationship, that is not true love. If a man loves you the right way, there should be no hesitation or questioning of his leadership in the household.

Many of my female clients get very upset at the mention of the word *submission*. It should not be a bad word. I don't believe God intended it to be a dirty word. It should be a word of honor and respect. It should represent love and security. Regardless of what the definition of it is, you have to define it for your own marriage. Man defined it, so man can alter it. God inspires the Bible. God does not inspire the dictionary. You have every right to make a word mean what you want it to mean. I have cleaned up the word *submission* as it relates to my household and marriage. To be honest, it doesn't even have to be mentioned; it just needs to be understood. Innately, we already understand it. Most women allow the man to lead. I have seen many women do crazy, irrational things for their men. We have to remove the blind submission and replace it with godly submission. We need this to be a two-way street filled with love and respect.

It takes a lot of strength to honor your vows and God's Word. It is not easy to overlook your desires all for the good of your household.

Who is the man worthy of your trust and honor? He should be a responsible man. This is the type of man who knows who he is and what he wants out of life. He is not easily influenced by the world around him. He's not chasing after his boys, going to the clubs, and getting drunk and high. This man isn't gambling away his life savings. He isn't immature and insecure. This type of man doesn't belittle others in an attempt to make himself feel big. He is not vindictive and bitter. He doesn't try to control and dictate. He's a man of honor, dignity, integrity, and respect. These attributes help you know that this man isn't out to hurt you or mislead you. He wants to see you win and win big. He wants to see you happy and living your best life. His children are his inspiration as well. He wants to set the best possible example for them. This is the type of man you can trust and support.

The issue with submission is that it has been abused over the years. It's been thrown around by undeserving men and then pinned on the Bible. An abusive man is quick to quote the Bible and the scriptures about submission. What he doesn't understand is that the concept is nullified if the man is not living in a God-like fashion. If the man isn't upholding his end of the bargain, submission is out the window. No wife should submit to a cheating man. No wife should submit to an abusive man, a selfish man, or an immature man. The word *submission* should be understood properly, and it should not be a weapon.

The benefits are great when love and trust are done the right way.

Allowing a man to lead his household builds his confidence and gives him a sense of purpose. The wife may be influencing every decision, but because she isn't flaunting, forcing, or demanding that influence, the man still feels like a leader. It gives a man purpose and allows him to live with his head held high.

A lot of women strip a man of his pride by attacking him verbally. On average, women are smarter than men. Women know that, and so do men. A woman who uses that to her advantage and makes her man feel stupid is destroying her relationship from the inside out. A broken man won't reach his full potential. Yes, breaking his spirit may make a woman feel like she's in charge of the home, but in the end, it will backfire. Don't give an abusive man any power or control, but if he is a loving man and honors his role, let him walk in it. Support and encourage him. It should not be a battle for leadership in the home. There should be a culture of mutual respect. God made things the way He did for a reason. He placed a natural guide within each of us. We have to take what's in us and use it to create healthy, loving homes. A woman naturally listens to the man she loves. A man naturally protects and provides for the woman he loves. Where we've gone wrong is by abusing the natural order of things. Men take advantage of a woman's willingness to submit. Women take advantage of a man's need to feel like the leader in his home. Men hurt women. Women hurt men. It's a vicious cycle that can be avoided if we just honor the instructions given to us. We can create long-lasting relationships that are healthy and beneficial to both parties.

Trust has to be at the center of every relationship. A man has to trust that his woman loves and honors him. A woman has to trust that her man loves and honors her. The two have to come together and use their strengths to make it work. Their children will be watching every move they make, which will teach them how to operate in their future relationships. Boys will learn how to become men, and girls will learn how to be women. Be careful about the example you set.

Change the narrative around submission. Erase the bad and painful things that have happened to you in the name of submission, and embrace God's mission for love. Both parties must be of one accord. There is nothing that we can't accomplish if we come together. Loving and respecting your spouse should be the main goal. If both of you keep that goal at the center, the relationship will work. If either of you deviates from the plan, it will fail.

Leadership is service, and submission is strength. It goes both ways, so know which side you're on in every situation. Accept the role you have to play as different events arise in life. Your role won't always be the same and it may switch daily, but you have to be okay with doing what you have to do to help make it work. Selfishness will ruin what you are trying to build. Don't get it twisted. This isn't to hurt you, control you, or anything of that nature. Keep walking in love.

Here are some things to think about:

1. Do you hate the word *submission*? If so, why?

2. Do you agree that *submission* has become a dirty word?

3. Do you think we should eliminate the word? If so, why?

4. Do you think we can clean the word up and operate in it the way God intended for us to? If not, why?

5. Have you ever been taken advantage of in the name of submission?

6. Submission takes strength.

7. Submission doesn't mean you should be a slave in your relationship.

8. Submission goes both ways.

9. Don't abuse your position in the relationship.

10. Trust, honor, and love.

eighteen

DON'T MIX LOVE WITH LUST

I have been paying close attention to couples in this day and time. The fast-paced society of today has made many people impatient and insatiable, especially millennials. Nothing is good enough for us. A $30,000 car isn't good enough; we want a $100,000 car. A $250,000 house isn't good enough; we want a $500,000 house. We don't want one lover; we want many. With everything we get, we want more, and nothing seems to satisfy our appetite. There has to be a way to reverse the course.

I have outlined four levels of love. There are lust, like, love, and self-love. Lust is the lowest form of love. It is a part of love, but by itself, it is not real love. Lust burns. Love warms. Lust eats us alive. Love keeps us alive. Lust can ruin you. Love can save you. Lust is very beneficial inside of a faithful marriage. Outside of marriage, it can be very dangerous. Now, more than ever, many are giving in to lust at alarming rates. It's so much easier to act on your lust today because of the internet. Pornography is free online. Instagram allows racy pictures, and dating apps and websites have made dating so much more accessible. You can sit at home and connect with someone from your phone and never set foot outside. People are meeting online, and some are even getting married. It's a thrill. It's fun. It's something new. More and more, people are growing insatiable for all things of pleasure. In every area of pleasure, there is an increase that I've noticed while working with individuals from around the world. It doesn't matter the age, race, or location; people are becoming more and more greedy and less satisfied with life.

A relationship must be between two people. Marriage must be the goal, and sex needs to occur within the confines of marriage. Many of us, including myself, have made mistakes with sex before marriage. I'll be the first to tell you how damaging it is. The knowledge I have acquired from it is why I advocate for abstinence until marriage. I believe in doing it God's way. I will not tell my two sons it is okay for them to experiment with sex before marriage. I will urge them to the best of my ability to do it God's way. I hope they listen.

It is so important that all sexual energy be given to your spouse. Do not sex-shame your spouse. Allow your spouse to be freely and deeply in love with you. Allow your spouse to feel extremely lustful for you and you only. Encourage it and reinforce it. So much good comes from it.

May your fountain be blessed, and may you rejoice in the wife of your youth. A loving doe, a graceful deer—may her breasts satisfy you always, may you ever be intoxicated with her love. Why, my son, be intoxicated with another man's wife? Why embrace the bosom of a wayward woman? For your ways are in full view of the LORD; and he examines all your paths.

—PROVERBS 5:18–21 (NEW INTERNATIONAL VERSION)

Lust and love can be a very intoxicating combination. If the two are combined the right way and kept sacred inside of marriage, the benefits are beyond comprehension. I am a living witness to this truth. The more you lust after your spouse and fulfill the love in your marriage, the stronger your bond becomes. If you also give attention to great communication, honesty, trust, and honor, your relationship can withstand the test of time. You will benefit greatly from giving all your love to one person, your spouse.

Your emotions will run high, and your feelings will grow deeper. Your love will be well rooted and very hard to tear from the foundation. Things work in your favor when you are in love in your marriage. Now, the insatiable desire grows for your spouse and not the things of the world. It fills you up and motivates you to live a fulfilled life. Your focus increases in the areas where you need it the most. Without the distractions of outside lust, you are able to focus on the important things outside of your marriage, like your purpose. You can fulfill your purpose because you have clarity surrounding your life. You increase your favor because you are in the right standing with God. Fulfill and express your love to the point you're satisfied. Those moments of lustful temptation will come and last for a day, and then the love will take back over and you'll want more quality time and expression of pure love. Love consumes you, but it also revives you if done inside of a healthy marriage.

You can't let anyone or anything come in between your love. It must be a priority, and everyone in your life must know the boundaries. On the day we dedicate to love, February 14, I don't even respond to text messages. That day is solely for my wife. Of course I love her and show it every day, but on the day the nation has dedicated to love, I let everyone know I take it very seriously. Ironically, I get a lot of text messages on that day because people want to see if I'm living what I'm teaching. Yes, I am. I love with everything inside me and without distraction. Love can be much stronger than you could even imagine. We take it for granted in most cases, but the true power of love is overwhelming at times. To keep things in balance, you have to periodically have some alone time. Alone time and time with your friends are essential while building this type of love.

Issues arise when you invite the wrong types of lust into your home. In all honesty, it's usually men who can't seem to keep their lust in bounds. Occasionally I encounter women who struggle with lust and fidelity. It can be as simple as masturbation. Yes, I went there; it's very real. The act of masturbation eventually takes you out of bounds because if it were about loving your spouse rather than physical lust, you would not need to engage in such an act. It takes you out of bounds because you eventually begin to lust after what you don't have. It makes no sense to commit the act because you can actually fulfill that lust in reality. The act of engaging in masturbation is a mental process that takes your mind out of bounds to visualize what you do not have in front of you. That is dangerous. In that context, lust grows and can't be quenched. You put yourself at risk of reenacting what happened in your mind, but in reality. You attract the wrong energy to your life. Your spouse should be all you need. If you feel the need to seek other sources of fulfillment, communication is lacking and that needs to be addressed.

Another major issue is pornography. This presents a similar issue because you begin to teach yourself that your partner's body and love aren't enough. You begin to fantasize and desire the physical touch of and intercourse with someone else. You can contain this in your mind for only so long. The human mind moves toward that which it focuses on. So if you are focusing on the sex of others, eventually the desire will become irresistible. I have coached many men who have confessed this to me, and many men have gone to therapy to treat their addiction to pornography. Some men struggled with it, overcame it, and went on to write and teach about it because the experience was just that real. It's very important to evaluate your mind-set around sex and intimacy. Identify the root of the issue and why you feel the need to entertain such acts. Why isn't your spouse enough? Why aren't you able to remain in bounds and rejoice in the love of your spouse? Addiction may feel natural to some people, but the mind is very powerful and can overcome this struggle if the desire is truly there. It may take therapy, prayer, fasting, and a support group. I have met countless individuals who claim to have overcome the addiction.

If you go without it, will it kill you? It may feel like it will, but it won't. You won't stop breathing. You may think about it all day and it will kill your focus, but it won't take your breath away. Your heart may race. You may sweat. You may have anxiety, but it will not stop you from breathing. If you're breathing and you're beating it in the moment, keep going. Pray without ceasing. Find an accountability partner. Find someone who has overcome the same problem and ask for guidance. Listen to their story, use their techniques, and then add your own.

It's very important that you fight the good fight. If you don't, one thing will lead to another. You will struggle, but the victory will be worth the war. You can win the fight if you make up your mind that you want to overcome.

Most of the time, you lose the fight because you have become addicted to both the pleasure and the instant gratification. The instant gratification you get from lust feels better to you than the love in your relationship. That is the case because you are not focusing on the love in your relationship. You have become distracted by lust and pleasure, and it has stolen your focus from your spouse. If you're lusting after another person on a computer or phone screen, you are not talking to your spouse. If you're not talking to your spouse, the bond between the two of you is weakening, while the bond between you and the screen is growing stronger. What you focus on grows. What you ignore dies. The same way you can grow lust is the same way you can kill it. If you ignore the screen and designate that time to your spouse, your lust for the screen will die and your love for your spouse will grow. You have to try it to believe it. You have to be committed to seeing it all the way through, and it will happen for you. It will work in your favor. If doing this doesn't work for you, there may be another issue in your relationship that needs to be addressed. Is it communication? Is it trust? Is it loyalty? Is it forgiveness? What is it that is pulling you further away from your spouse and closer to the screen? You will have to create a plan to win this war. If you can't create it, hire a professional to help you create it. You will have to assign every hour of your day to doing something productive. You won't be able to let an hour tell you what to do. You will have to tell the hour how you will be spending it. Time will become yours, and you have to manage it wisely. There will have to be prayer in your day. Meditation will need to be added to your day. Physical exercise can fill a space as well. Constant communication with your spouse is required. Special times that are reserved for your spouse must be on your schedule. No time can be idle. Fight the good fight, and win this spiritual war.

Some couples I have coached took their sexual dysfunction beyond masturbation and pornography. They even went as far as the physical.

The next step is strip clubs. There is brokenness throughout the building. The person who owns the club operates from brokenness and a desire for money. They know they can get rich from the brokenness and confusion of others. The dancers, and I've coached many, have a desire for something different but are battling the unspeakable in their lives. They are hurting. They are lost. They are confused. Some adapt to the environment and grow a thick skin to mask their problems. Some normalize the lifestyle and pretend the way they make a living is perfectly okay. If that were the truth, they would never leave it for other opportunities like reality television and music careers. The hurt, pain, and confusion are running all through the building. The patrons who frequent the strip club are dealing with the same type of confusion. They are running from their problems and seeking pleasure to fill the void and mask the pain. They do not want to face their nightmares. They do not want to confront their pain. They do not want to deal with their issues. It's an escape. It's a high. They get lost in the moment and are adamant that they are living life to the fullest. I've coached them, too. I've coached many individuals who are normal by most accounts. They work great jobs. They look professional and dress professionally. They have a clean image and a clean name, yet they find themselves in a strip club reinforcing the women on the poles.

At some point in my coaching career it was brought to my attention that there are clubs you can go to and watch other people have sex. Anyone can get naked, get into a bed, and have sex. Patrons visit these places and stand around watching others have sex as if they were wild animals in a zoo. The people in these clubs are not deranged people ready to jump off a cliff. These people are your idols, your celebrities, professional athletes, actors, realtors, bankers, and so on. There is a movement, and has always been a movement in certain pockets of society, to normalize these things. Couples visit these places and expect it to enhance their relationship. It does the exact opposite. In over a decade of relationship coaching, I have never met a truly happy couple that engages in these acts. I have not met one successful, happily married couple who has been together for more than a decade and partakes in this lifestyle. I meet couples who are just getting started and don't know any better. They haven't had enough time to experience the repercussions of taking lust out of bounds. I've met couples who appear to be happy, but truthfully, the woman is usually broken and disguising her pain just to keep her man around. The man is actually lost and confused but doesn't want to admit it because he feels it would make him appear less than a man.

If these things could benefit a relationship, I would be recommending them. They do not help, and if they do, it's all an illusion. It's temporary, and it will fade. Last, it will destroy the relationship. Eventually someone grows tired of the lifestyle and starts verbalizing his or her desire for normalcy. The person may not even realize it, but he or she is actually trying to get closer to what God has called him or her to do. Lust out of bounds causes a lot of pain. It deepens confusion and worsens pain. The lust grows, and it turns into a monster. It enables one person and devours the other. One person in the relationship uses it to his or her benefit, while the other person suffers quietly. Typically, this lifestyle comes about after a man tries to convince a woman that it's not natural to be faithful. He tells her he can never be faithful and won't pretend to be able to be faithful. He asks her for her respect so he can toss it into the trash. There is no desire to truly love the woman, but instead, the desire is to use her. This man is lost, confused, and hurting, but rather than face those issues, he's ready to create more. He is going to ruin her heart and mind just as his have been ruined. He was never shown a better way, so he's just living life to the best of his ability. He's caught up in the snare of pleasure, failing to realize that chasing pleasure will lead to more pain. All he wants to do is fix his hurting heart, but he's turning to vices instead of to his creator. Only God can make a man new and whole. If the man doesn't realize that, he self-destructs. He ends up living a miserable existence until his untimely death. If you look at many of our celebrities who have fallen into this lifestyle, you can see the self-destruction. There is no peace in sex, drugs, and lies. That lifestyle does not sustain a relationship; it *destroys* a relationship.

There are many who claim not to be as extreme. They don't snort drugs, smoke a lot, or drink a lot; they claim they are just having a good time. They work great jobs, and some even go to church, but according to their notions, this unbridled lust helps their relationship. They look around and see very few successful couples, so they are winging it their own way. They have seen men and women try to keep things in bounds and fail. They see 50 percent of marriages fail, and the statistics are even worse for second and third marriages. That convinces them to try it this way and give in to untamed lust.

The lust starts slow. It entertains. It entices. It excites. It revitalizes and invigorates. Then it begins its slow creep. It begins to spread. The lust spreads to the body, mind, and spirit. It moves like a cancer throughout the body. Eventually, lust that exists outside of your marriage will destroy something. It will destroy your mind, your body, your relationship, or all three. It doesn't come to play nice. It comes to take over. The lust leads to strong desires that extend beyond your spouse. It makes you want a different body type, a different smile, a different smell, and other things that your spouse doesn't possess. In most cases, it starts with a woman trying to let her man "be a man," but truthfully, she's giving him room to be less than a man. She's trying to keep him happy, unaware of the fact that his happiness does not lie in her power. Humans can't keep other humans happy. Happiness is a choice, and it has to be found within. A choice has to be made, and happiness cannot be contingent upon circumstances or experiences. This woman is providing experiences to keep him happy, but they are destroying him instead. A man can't lie in fire and not be burned. He will be burned, eventually he will be consumed, and so will she if she's lying next to him.

The couple begins to lust more and more, and now just looking at the dancers is not enough. There needs to be some physical touch. The mind will demand that the fantasy become reality. That is when many couples, even some who claim to love God, begin to have sex outside of their marriage. I have coached couples who do threesomes and foursomes on Saturday night and then go to church on Sunday morning. Yes, many believe that this can be a part of a healthy relationship. It is everything but healthy. Things get physical. Now that someone has been invited into your bed, your bed is defiled. A soul tie has been created, and because it's out of bounds, it will wreak havoc on the relationship. Something happens. The man starts to desire the outside woman alone. He wants her to himself. Sometimes the woman starts to desire the outside woman to herself. The outside woman catches feelings and starts to desire one of them. The third leg makes things very unstable. The excitement the couple was seeking is about to take over and turn into a disaster.

We are human. We have feelings. Our feelings must be contained and used in productive, healthy ways. If we step out of bounds, our feelings will destroy us because they take over and we self-destruct. The mind gets a high from pleasure. The chemicals the brain releases become addictive. These same chemicals can be released with lust in bounds, but if it's out of bounds, it works against you. You can't control the feelings of another human being. Those feelings can become suicidal or homicidal, and in many cases, that is what happens. The Bible says the wages of sin is death. It means that if you venture too far into sin, it will eventually cost you your life. It happens every time.

In coaching, I have found that many women lose themselves in these types of relationships. They begin to hurt, feel anger, jealousy, and rage. Then they are on edge at all times. Anxiety sets in because they have heard stories of men leaving their women for a dancer they met together at a strip club. Now what was supposed to help the relationship hurts the relationship. Investing time and energy into ungodly lust is dangerous. It may have a little return right away, but eventually you will lose it all. I've watched couple after couple fail in this type of relationship. Some last a decade but have been reeling since year two. They've been holding on, trying to prove to themselves and to the world that they can do it their way and make it work. They want to prove so badly that a couple can engage in all forms of lustful activities outside of marriage and not be hurt by it. But it's a futile effort.

The woman rages with love for the man. The man slowly loses interest in the woman and wants to replace her with a new main woman and a new side woman. His lust can't be quenched because he feeds it daily. It's getting stronger and more demanding. It wants more and more. It becomes a game. It's fun to him, but it's slowly destroying him. Eventually the lust runs over into other areas of his life and turns him to other vices. It's typically drugs, alcohol, or gambling. He has trained his brain to seek a thrill, and now he can't stop. If he doesn't know any better, he doesn't even have the desire to stop. Doing it the right way makes no logical sense because he has never seen the benefits of it. He doesn't know me, and when he hears of me, he doesn't believe my reasoning. He tells himself that I am saying what I'm saying for money and that I probably cheat on my wife all the time. He's trying to convince himself that his way is the only way and nothing else is real. He's hurting, lost, and confused. It will take traumatic life events to wake him up. That may be the hardship of being deserted by every woman he tries to loop into his game. If enough women catch on to his brokenness and turn him over to God, maybe he will have no other choice. But there always seems to be at least one more woman who is willing to give this wild ride a try.

You can't invite the Devil into your home and not expect him to take over. Lust will wreak havoc on your life if you let it. It will take more from you than you can afford to lose. It will cost you more than you can replace. It's important to understand the power of lust and use it to your benefit in your marriage and only with your spouse. If you can keep lust and love in bounds, it will strengthen your relationship beyond understanding. You will be so deeply in love with your spouse that doing a term of life together will not be a hard thing to ask. It will be rewarding along the way. Your struggles will look easy to others and feel easy to you because true love is just that powerful.

Don't be tricked into doing what the rest of the world is doing. Lean on and trust in the blueprint for healthy love. Make love revolve around your spouse and nothing else. Keep love in bounds, and indulge in it. Let it make you stronger. Keep finding ways to love deeper, and don't turn your back on real love. You will see people flaunt different types of relationships, and some will brag on them out of ignorance. But be not moved. They are bragging about their sexcapades, not because it's healthy but because they are trying to convince themselves that they're okay. If they can convince you to try it and to believe that it's healthy and normal, it validates their actions and keeps the cycle of confusion going. One day there will be enough evidence and enough real confessions to show that this is not the way to go. If you have to lose yourself to keep someone else happy, you are in the wrong relationship. Pack your bags, and run like crazy.

Here are some things to think about:

1. Have you ever let lust get the best of you?

2. Have you ever stepped outside of your relationship? If so, what happened?

3. Do you believe strong lust for your spouse can be dangerous? If so, why?

4. If you don't lust after your spouse, do you feel something is wrong? If so, why?

5. Do you think it's ever okay to let your spouse step outside of the relationship? If so, why?

6. If your spouse asked you for permission to step outside of the relationship, what would your answer be? Why?

7. Lust out of bounds will destroy your marriage.

8. It is not normal or healthy to invite a third party into your bed.

9. If you have to lose yourself to keep someone, that's not love.

10. Lust, unlike thirst, cannot be quenched.

nineteen

WORK TOGETHER

Work together *literally*, meaning do business together. This may sound like the same thing as being teammates, but it is a different angle. One thing I have noticed in my own relationship and coaching others is that couples who work together are typically happy. It may do more for one person than the other, but it still works. There is a bond that is formed when two people work together in some capacity. There is strength in differences. If you can work together with your spouse, the two of you complement each other. You think with one side of your brain and your partner with the other. You may see things your spouse can't see and vice versa.

Some of the most successful couples run businesses together. If it is done the right way, you are able to push and inspire each other. There will be disagreements and misunderstandings, but that's where the other chapters come into play. You have become teammates, you have picked a captain in each area of work, and now you're working together in reality to make it work. Working together can take you a long way.

It can be simply exercising together. You have probably heard that couples that pray together, stay together. That is both true and not true. There are always exceptions to the rules. Working out together can bring you closer, and you push each other to greatness. It's inspiring to see your spouse getting fit and sexy. It works in your favor. Some people start affairs in the gym. You won't have to worry about that if you work out with your spouse. The beauty of this teamwork is that it puts you on the same life path. Imagine how imbalanced it would feel if one of you became super fit and the other completely gave up. At that point, you won't be on the same page and it will hurt the relationship. Do something simple like working out together. Make a plan for it, and make it happen at least once a week. Make this time a no-argument time. Be the bigger person, roll with the punches, go with the flow, and be committed to having a good time together. As your spouse sees your positive and upbeat attitude, he or she will know he or she has to vibe on the same frequency for it to be fulfilling. Don't let it turn into a negative experience. Working out together will give you mental, emotional, and physical release. You're boosting your libido, increasing your life expectancy, and bonding at the same time.

There may be some frustrations that hold you back from working out with your spouse. Get over it. It's a part of growth. Maybe the other person goes too hard in workouts. Maybe they want to yell or motivate too much. Maybe they're lazy and quit easily. Love those quirks about your spouse, and learn to work around them. After all, you are in it for the long haul with this person. If you can't stand to work out together, how long can you last? Push yourself, and make it happen. It may have the same effect on both of you mentally and emotionally, or it may be better for one of you. This is quality time. If quality time is very important to one of you, it's going to push the love meter to the top. Your wife will be head over heels. It's that easy sometimes. We often wonder how we can get more out of our partners. You have to give more to get more. If you give more time and have fun in that time, it will better your relationship. If you speak to your spouse's heart in a way that really matters to him or her, he or she will love you more. Even if it's a sacrifice for you to make this time happen, it will pay off in the long run.

It can go deeper than just working out together. Start a venture together, or start a business for each of you. Start a company together and divide the workload, put your heads together, and make it work. Identify your strengths, and make sure you're operating in your strengths and not your weaknesses. Maybe you're already doing this. If so, look around and see how it works for other couples. Notice what they do right and what they do wrong. Learn from the successes and mistakes of others, and let it help you. Couples have tried this, but sometimes it fails because they aren't doing the other important things, like communicating effectively and being faithful to each other. Perhaps they are just in business together and money is the motive. Make sure it's deeper than money. Work with a purpose, and push each other to greatness. Know your strengths and play to them. Don't try to force something on your spouse that doesn't fit. Your husband may not be an entrepreneur; don't try to force him to start a company. You start the company and give him a role within the company that fits his personality. There may be opportunities out there for him to start a business and succeed, but if he's not into it, you cannot force him. You do your thing, and appreciate his love and support in the areas where his skills shine. Your wife may be a little bossy. Let her take control of a part of the business where you know she'll flourish. Submit to her in that area, and let her run it. She's stronger than you in that area, so don't let your ego get in the way of success. Let her handle it. Delegate authority, and let it run the way it should.

Business can work if you work it. Don't stand in the way of your success by letting your personality differences hinder you. You're teammates, so work together. Many financial experts teach that it's important to have multiple streams of income. Each of us has some type of gift that could potentially build additional earnings. If both of you have areas where you can win, support each other. The husband may run a motivational speaking business, and the wife may run a T-shirt line. The wife can manage the husband's speaking career, answer emails, and read contracts. The husband can help the wife brainstorm T-shirt designs, share feedback, and assist in pressing the shirts. Now you have two businesses in which both of you are hands-on. You're in your strong zone and making it work. The two of you are supporting each other and discovering ways to enhance and expand both businesses. There are major benefits to this. You can make money, make love, have fun, and grow together. You don't have to worry about the other person having an extramarital affair on the job, because you're working together. You learn to love each other more because you have to work together and then sleep together.

This can be amazing if you want it to work. One of the greatest lessons you will learn from this is getting over yourself. Your spouse will probably want to do something you have no interest in doing. Become interested in it, and help the team win. You will want to do something that does not interest your spouse at all. If you are helping him, he will help you. If your spouse won't support you, that's a sign you need to see before it's too late. Get to the bottom of that issue immediately. You can't thrive with someone who does not want to support you.

Include each other in starting businesses, and be faithful to each other in every area of your life. This will help your family earn more money and create a safety net, and it may even enable you to retire from a job where you work for someone else. Couples are learning that they work better together rather than working with someone else outside of the marriage. Think about the magnitude of working with someone you know has your best interests at heart, of knowing you are working toward the common goal of feeding the same household. When you work with someone else, there could be more competition and less loyalty. That person may be trying to get whatever they can from you and not care how it affects you. With a spouse, you are literally working together and on the same team. You are sleeping in the same bed, eating the same food, and spending the same money. Being successful both in and out of business should be the ultimate goal, because you have a long life together ahead of you.

It's not a flawless operation; there are some issues that come into play with this notion. Some couples let the success and results of working together get in the way. Look at a simple example. Imagine you are working out with your spouse, and his or her body starts responding faster than yours does. If her body gets supersexy and you're still working with a keg instead of a six-pack, some problems could arise. If communication is lacking and healing from the past is still pending, the problem can ruin your relationship. Her nice body may get her a lot of new attention. It could make you insecure and you may start mistreating her for no reason. You begin questioning her loyalty, and she gets tired of it. She becomes distant, and then another man on her job starts talking to her at lunch. He's tall, handsome, fit, and very nice. He starts to fill a void, and she's allowing it because she never saw it coming. It's also hap-

pening because her hurt feelings from her treatment at home have left
her vulnerable; it's like ointment on a wound she's nursing. The next
thing you know, an affair is happening. The results of the work got in
the way because all the other pieces weren't in play. If there had been
healthy communication and the work had been done, this could have
been avoided.

It's important to make sure you have the work in place. Make sure
every piece of the puzzle is in place. Even in an actual business, money
can be a problem. You can start making large amounts of money in the
business you're in with your spouse. Then one of you lets it go to your
head. You're splurging on the finer things in life, and you start feeling
yourself in a new way. You're a success now. You forgot the days when
the two of you struggled together. Now that you're successful, you think
you could have done it on your own. Your feelings start to change. The
pain of the past is still burning, and now that money is involved, you realize you can walk away with half and do just fine.

Don't let the results of your hard work ruin the work you've done.
While you are working together to build your relationship, make sure
you actually do the other work to keep things intact. Keep communication at the top of your list. Be 100 percent faithful in mind, body, and
spirit. Have discernment about who and what you entertain. Don't get
sidetracked by distractions that only come to hurt you. Remain focused
on the ultimate goal. You are building a relationship to make it work,
not to tear it apart. Never let your mind play tricks on you and convince
you that you can be better on your own, especially if you know you have
a good person by your side who loves you wholeheartedly. Don't take his
or her kindness for granted. It does not matter what small flaws you'd
like to be changed. If changing them won't lead to something positive,

ignore them. It's important that you don't let the results of your work shine a negative light on things you would otherwise have overlooked. Keep things in perspective.

Serve the world together. We are all familiar with the term *power couple*. Be a power couple. Make a plan, and make things happen. Serve the world, and support each other along the journey. Others will try to come between you. They will try to be your partner in business and replace your spouse. Always listen to the voice of the one who loves you. Even if you do not physically or literally work in the same company, at least hear your spouse's voice and respect his or her input. Your spouse wants to see you win. That's what this is about. Do the practical things that will bring you closer and strengthen your bond. Every day that you give love a chance to grow, the more it does. The more time you spend with your spouse working on yourself and your relationship, the stronger you become. The more hours you put in, the better prepared you will be for the real test. If you have no bond, tough times will tear you apart. If you have a strong bond, nothing can come between you.

Know where you stand in your spouse's heart, and don't drop the ball. Don't allow anyone to step in and do what you should be doing. What you won't do, someone else will. Always remember that. If you start taking shortcuts, you will get cut short. There is always someone waiting in the wings for you to slip up. Don't slip up. Don't just be teammates; actually work together and build something special.

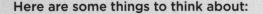

Here are some things to think about:

1. Have you ever worked with your spouse? What were the benefits, if any?

2. Would it be impossible for you to work with your spouse? If so, why?

3. If someone else came along to do the job of your spouse, would you replace your spouse? Why or why not?

4. What would be the cons of working with your spouse, if any?

5. Do you believe in the term *power couple*? Why or why not?

6. Can a relationship work if your spouse doesn't support your business? If so, how will you make it work?

7. You don't have to have a business together to have a happy relationship.

8. Work together in some capacity to strengthen your relationship.

9. Support your spouse in his or her endeavors.

10. Don't let the work hinder the relationship.

twenty

FIND BALANCE

A healthy relationship has all sorts of moving parts. It takes a lot of work and effort to reach the place you need to be in your relationship. There must be trust. There must be communication. There must be honesty. There must be loyalty. The list of necessities is long. Most of the elements you need will fall into place with communication and honesty. If you have those two, the rest will come naturally. It's great to be close, but you cannot become completely dependent on your spouse.

First, you have to dedicate enough time to your spouse so he or she falls deeply in love with you and builds trust with you. Your spouse needs to be comfortable with you so the truth can flow from his or her mouth without hesitation. You two have to know each other well enough that you're not easily offended. The more time you spend together and the closer you become, the better you'll know each other. You've heard the song that says, "If you don't know me by now, you will never, never, never know me." That's true of lots of relationships because some couples don't spend enough time together. Imagine being married to someone who has to travel out of state every week. It's really hard to build a relationship with someone who is physically in a different place so often. It may take twice the amount of time or longer to gain true knowledge of a person in a situation like that. Imagine the relationships of professional athletes. Being a life coach to pro athletes, I see the challenges firsthand. A lot of athletes are closer to their teammates than they are to their spouses. There's so much time spent with the team and so many more experiences shared. In some cases, their hearts grow fonder for their teams than for their spouses. That makes it challenging to share true love and real trust. But a way has to be made.

You must find a way to be independent when you need to be, even though a relationship is interdependent. Many people become codependent. The danger in codependency is that you feel like nobody without your spouse around.

Codependent: of or relating to a relationship in which one person is physically or psychologically addicted, as to alcohol or gambling, and the other person is psychologically dependent on the first in an unhealthy way. (www.dictionary.com)

The definition of *codependent* is pretty serious. Some call it love, but that's what I call dangerously in love. That is not healthy for the long haul. It can drive you insane if your existence depends on your partner's existence. That's why it is imperative that you fix yourself first. Do the work to learn, heal, forgive, and grow. Heal from the pain of your past. Heal from the abuse, abandonment, hurt, and pain. Gain new knowledge, and grow from those past experiences. Hire a therapist and life coach if you need professional insight and assistance in your process of healing. Make the investment in yourself, and get the help you need. It's very dangerous to depend on another human being for validation.

Interdependent: mutually dependent; depending on each other. (www.dictionary.com)

There is a difference between codependence and interdependence. Interdependence can create a healthy marriage. You're depending on each other to show up in the relationship and each do your part, but not in an unhealthy way. If your counterpart does not show up, it won't kill you. It will hurt you, but you know who you are and what you bring to the table. The goal is to be interdependent. Once you reach that level, you've gained the maturity and readiness for a healthy, long-lasting relationship. If you are not interdependent, keep learning and growing.

There is a time for balance. In the beginning, you may need to focus solely on your spouse. The two of you are focused on each other, and you're building a bond that can't be broken. After that season, you're able to find more space independent of the other. You can separate because you know, love, and trust each other. It's similar to being best friends. You may have someone whom you consider a best friend, but you don't speak to that person every day. You may let a month pass without talking, but when you talk, it's like you never missed a beat. That's a best friend. Well, you will be even closer than that with your spouse. However, remember that you are human. It can get bothersome to have only one person to lean on. If there is no one else, you must create someone else. If you focus on being a good friend, you will attract good friends. Join a life group at your church. Get involved, and meet people. It's necessary. It's not attractive to brag about having no friends other than your spouse. You may build relationships that will be classified not as "best friends" but as associates and acquaintances. Associates can be demoted or fired. That's okay, but you need to have other outlets. Isolation is never good. Have someone you can talk to about your interests and passions.

Step out with the guys for a guys' night out. Step out with the girls for a girls' night out. Meet other couples, and have one couples night a month and one guys' and girls' night out. Develop friendships at work and/or church. There are conversations that are better had with a friend than with your spouse. Save your spouse some of the trouble by having other people you can talk to about things that are in their areas of expertise. As a husband, you may be passionate about business. Your wife may not be that into business. If you have a good guy friend you can call and have lunch with to talk about all the new trends in business, that conversation will be much more fulfilling than boring your spouse about it. As a wife, you may be into fashion and decorating. If you have a good girlfriend you can call and talk to about the latest fashion and design, that conversation will be much more fulfilling than boring your husband with the details. It could also be the other way around. As a wife you may be focused on building your business, but your husband is okay working for someone else and may not care to talk about business. Yes, it is important that you develop some interest in the things that interest your spouse, but you don't have to be the only person he or she can speak to about it. Encourage your spouse to spend time with friends. Get into that healthy space, and create a night out. Create space to give both of you time to miss each other. Find time to compare stories with others and build with other people. Of course, you want to make sure the people you build with are like-minded. It wouldn't be smart to be best friends with a person who doesn't believe in maintaining a relationship and making it work. You need wise counsel, not the opposite.

If you feel some jealousy around this topic, explore the reasons why. If a man is falling short in the relationship and his woman is hanging out with her girlfriends, he fears her friends will get the scoop and advise his woman to leave him. That's a valid fear to have. You should create the scenario so it will light a fire under you to get your act together. Even if you try to isolate your spouse, eventually he or she will get out and confide in someone. At some point, someone will hear his or her cries. So instead of trying to trap your spouse in the house, become a better person and love the right way.

Another reason you may not like this idea is that you feel you already don't get enough time with your spouse as it is. Well, express that. How much time do you need from your spouse, and are your expectations realistic? Do you need more time than the average healthy-minded person does? Do you need more time because you're trying to fill a void? Why do you need more time? If it's a legitimate need, it needs to be expressed and plans need to be made to modify how much time is spent together. Remember, this is your relationship, too. Put yourself on your spouse's calendar. You come first. Don't *ask* your spouse for a date night on Friday night; *tell* him you are going on a date on Friday night. Tell him to put his phone down when he gets home from work. Let him know that it's your time and he needs to honor that. Business can wait. The emails and text messages can wait. Your marriage cannot wait. It's about you right now. Let it be known and demand your time. Get your fill, and then be open to your spouse having time outside of you.

Another reason some people are resistant to a partner's spending time away from the marriage is that the spouse always comes home acting differently. That's a valid concern. The reason is typically because of the conversation held with the friend. A lot of times, we have things on our chests that we want to say, but instead of saying them to our spouses, we voice them to others. Then we get the answer we want to hear, and it makes us resent our spouse for not being perfect. We're irritated because we expect our partner to already know what we want and need. It just doesn't work like that. Each of us has to learn this. Think about what you want to tell your friend about your spouse. Think it all the way through. Write it down if you need to. Then make the time to say it to your spouse. Don't forget to ask your spouse what is needed from you. There's probably something on his or her chest, too. This is the real communication we need in marriage. If it is taken care of in the home, there should be no need for negative venting when out with friends. In most cases, both parties are guilty of gossip, but sometimes one person knows how to hide it better. Handle business in the home so the time spent with friends can be fun and positive.

You may notice that your spouse comes home extremely happy after being out with friends. No, it does not mean he or she was cheating. It's no reason to be jealous. Don't get upset because you feel like you don't make your spouse that happy. You catch an attitude and tell your spouse that maybe he or she should date his or her best friend because the friend seems to make him or her happier. That's petty and counterproductive. You have to understand that time spent with friends is a different type of release. If you allow yourself to have friends, you know the feeling. It's a no-judgment zone. With friends, we don't have to worry about being criticized or getting into an argument. We aren't sleeping with our friends, so the tension isn't there. A friend can say something sharp, but we let it roll off our back. A spouse can say the same thing, and it turns into an argument. The difference is, we aren't seeking the love and approval of our friends, so we don't take offense at their opinions as deeply. We are seeking the love and approval of our spouse, so we take everything he or she says to heart. With our friends, we can relax all the way because the element of physical attraction is removed. Being free in that way relaxes the body and brings calm. On the other hand, being with a spouse makes us conscious of our appearance, and it creates tension or anxiety in the body. That can be draining if you're trying to suck your stomach in, turn your head so the other person doesn't smell the garlic on your breath, hold in the gas you need to let out, and so on. That can make for a painful experience. That is why building together and really getting to know each other is so important.

Some couples are still dating ten years into their relationship. That's both a good and a bad thing. The good thing is that they still get the butterflies on date night. The bad thing is that they may not be fully ready to give up their quality time with their spouse to friends. That is okay, because the time will come when the hair can be let down and the guys' and girls' nights can begin. A woman may be ten years into her relationship and still holding in gas, about to die. That's okay. The butterflies are still there, and she really loves and admires her man. One day, she will break wind and he will fall deeper in love with her, and she'll wonder why she's been killing herself all this time. A man may still be afraid to talk in close proximity to his wife because of the fear that his breath is off. He doesn't want the garlic smell to turn her off. That's fine. One day, she will smell his breath, make a face, cover her nose, and they'll both laugh it off. That will bring them closer, and he may blow dragon breath a little more often. That's love. This is life. We live and we learn. We grow as we go. You can't rush your relationship; neither can you force anything to happen. Let the natural occur, and always address the findings.

Get to a strong place in your relationship so you can have a life outside of your spouse. You will know when you're where you need to be. You will know when you and your spouse can be together and be absolutely in love but you can also take friend vacations without each other and miss each other in a healthy way. You can be happy that your spouse is getting some time without you. The two of you are also being 100 percent faithful while apart from each other. That is love. That is healthy love. Create some distance at times, and miss each other in a healthy way. When you come back together, each time will be like another honeymoon. It will feel fresh and new because you had some time apart. Be creative. Have fun. A relationship has to last a long time. Don't burn yourself out by trying to be everything to your spouse and nothing to anyone else. Don't put yourself on an island in isolation. Yes, it's important to keep your important business in-house, but you need to find balance and have healthy relationships outside of your spouse.

You and your spouse may feel some jealousy toward the other person's friends. Voice those concerns, and provide an opportunity to have the concerns silenced. If you feel a certain friend is a negative influence and you have proof, not just speculation, you have a right to speak on that. If it is confirmed that a friend is a bad influence, that friend must be cut off. There has to be a clear-cut distance created from that friend. Yes, friends are important, but let no one come before your relationship. So if a friend wants to take your husband to a strip club, he is a bad friend. If a friend wants to take your wife to a strip club, she is a bad friend. If a friend wants to go do some heavy gambling, get high and drunk and other things of that nature, that's a terrible friend. If you are trying to build a relationship God's way, your influences must be God-like influences.

Find balance, but do it the smart and healthy way. Communicate, communicate, communicate. That is the key to finding balance and creating a healthy, long-lasting relationship.

Here are some things to think about:

1. Do you truly have balance in your relationship?

2. Have you ever disliked your spouse's friends? If so, why?

3. Do you think it's important to have free time with friends? If so, what are the benefits for you?

4. Have you ever felt suffocated in a relationship? If so, what was the result of it?

5. Can you trust your spouse with his or her friends? If not, why?

6. Does your spouse like your friends? If not, why?

7. A healthy balance is nonnegotiable in relationships.

8. Isolation is not good.

9. It's great to have friends, but they must be good friends.

10. If you don't like your spouse's friends, have you identified and expressed why you don't?

twenty-one

CHECK YOUR FRIENDS

There are some things that arise with having friends that can ruin relationships. There are levels to a relationship, and the more comfortable you get in the relationship, the more chances you may take. However, you still have to be smart about your associations. There are various types of friends you have to avoid.

Affairs are not started in the bedroom; they start in conversations. A lot of couples try to have friends they find attractive. You can say you're a mature adult and you know how to have friends without crossing the line, but this situation is always a risk. As a husband, you can't have a female friend in the real sense of a friend. By friend, I mean a confidante. You can't confide in a female friend other than your wife. That type of communication is dangerous. The more you communicate, the more love you express. It's one thing to confide in a male friend because that has no risk of materializing into anything sexual. To confide in a woman is a totally different situation. The same rule applies to wives. A wife can't have a male friend as a confidant, because that man may sense vulnerability and make a move at some point. If you are in a situation like this, the friendship needs to come to an end.

This is a touchy subject because many couples make the argument that they have friends of the opposite sex, and the friendships were established prior to the marriage. It's totally understandable to want to maintain those friendships, but it doesn't make it any less dangerous or toxic. A friend is a human being with feelings. If your friend is attracted to you in any way, he or she can't help but give biased advice if you take relationship issues to him or her. The other thing you have to be honest about is if your friend has ever made a pass at you. If your friend has expressed his or her attraction to you in any way, it's inappropriate to remain friends with that person once you're married. You may have a person you call a friend, but you hear from the person only on holidays and your birthday. That is not a friend. That person does not fit the definition. However, if the person is someone with whom you share a romantic past, the friendship must be discontinued.

Don't play with fire. Yes, you're mature. Yes, you have it under control. You still must be smart. You have to cut ties with those individuals you once had feelings for or the other way around. Those feelings will blow up in your face if you allow them to linger. It may take ten or fifteen years to happen, but it will happen if you know there are feelings there. It's great to have friendships, but they have to be situations where sex is not a temptation and never has been.

A real friend will know his or her place. If a single man has a female friend and she gets married, he should expect his role to be eliminated. Yes, he could have been a platonic friend, but he knows that if the right opportunity presented itself, something sexual could happen. Affairs happen with so-called friends every day. They happen because the two individuals have been friends for so long and spent so much time building their relationship. Friendship is a strong foundation in a relationship, so it's dangerous grounds if you're friends with someone you could be with intimately. The friendship has been there for years, but maybe the two felt like they couldn't be a couple. So they just keep building together, falling in love in a friendly way all along. Then years later, after all this pent-up love is about to explode, a moment of vulnerability presents itself and one bold person makes the move. The other may let it happen because neither of them knows if they are actual soul mates. I have seen marriages end because one party befriended someone he or she could be attracted to and that attraction prevailed. I've seen men walk out on their wives and children because they claim their female friends are actually their soul mates. I've seen women do the same thing. Typically, those relationships fail, but you can't tell them that. It's dangerous ground to tread. Your friends should be in a safe zone and not people you can be attracted to in any way.

There are some people who say, yes, I have a friend of the opposite sex, but he or she isn't my type. That's not a good enough excuse. Sex is sex. Sex is emotional. People have sex with people they aren't physically attracted to every day. If the situation presents itself the right way or catches you in a moment of vulnerability, you will fall. You're honestly not that strong. You're not Jesus. Don't play yourself trying to prove a point to your spouse. You're human, and human beings cannot engage in inappropriate relationships without mishap.

The other aspect of such friendships is that your spouse may not be comfortable with a friend you have because your spouse believes that friend is attractive to you and believes you may fall for the friend. In a marriage, you have to honor that feeling. You can't keep a friend your spouse is 100 percent against. Trust your spouse's intuition. You may call your husband or wife jealous, insecure, crazy, or any other name to dismiss his or her instinct on the matter, but deep down, you know he or she has a valid point. If you try too hard to combat the point, one day you will be faced with the same choice, and it may cost your marriage. You have to ask yourself why you want to hold on to this risky friendship so badly. What is there to salvage? Is your friend the one you truly love? Be honest with yourself, and then be honest with your spouse.

The Bible says that a man will leave his mother and father and cleave to his wife. If we are expected to create distance from our parents upon our marriage, how much more should you be willing to create distance from an inappropriate friendship? It doesn't make sense to try to hold on to someone who makes your spouse uncomfortable. You have to make a choice: Do you want to be a friend in someone's friend zone, or do you want to be married? Or do you want to marry your friend? Tell yourself the tough truth.

It is understood that you will have colleagues and coworkers you may have to talk to on the phone in some capacity. Some of those people may be attracted to you, or you may find them attractive. Those relationships have to be navigated wisely. Do you really have to speak to those people outside of the workplace? What type of communication are you having? How often is the communication? Through what medium is the communication? What time of day or night is the communication? Those factors matter, and they are where the boundaries have to be set. You may have clients of the opposite sex, and you have to make sure those clients respect your relationship. Just because they are clients doesn't mean they are not attracted to you or not waiting for an opportunity to derail your relationship. Yes, it can happen, and yes, that is the goal of some people. You may be innocent and have pure intentions, but not everyone has pure intentions; therefore, you must be extremely cautious. To work with someone who has to communicate with you outside of work hours about work is one thing. To be friends with the person where attraction could play a role is a totally different issue. Don't lie to yourself.

It sounds very suspicious to a spouse if his or her partner is defending a friendship that seems to be risky. It raises a lot of concern and will drive a wedge in the relationship. It could very well be the undoing of the relationship. Is it worth that? Are you willing to risk it all for this person you're calling a friend? If so, I hope it's really worth the risk, but I seriously doubt that it is. There may be some exceptions to the rule. If you have found one in your relationship, only you know that. I'm sure there are some circumstances where people can have friends of the opposite sex where there is some type of attraction but it's never acted on or explored. Well, let me stop lying. I do not believe that. I have heard both men and women argue that their friendship with a person of the opposite sex is completely platonic. Then as I dug deeper, I'd ask if the friend had ever given them compliments about their looks or said something like "If only your boyfriend or girlfriend knew how amazing you are." I was able to identify times the friend had made a subtle pass but it was ignored or brushed off. The attraction is there. The friend shot his or her shot, but it was blocked. That didn't make the feelings evaporate. The friend is just waiting for the right time to shoot another shot. There is a lot of love in all those hours of conversation. A lot of time has been invested, and a lot of feelings are in the mix. It's only so much time a person can sit on the sidelines, and watch you love someone else, when deep down they feel they are the one for you.

Ironically, I have never seen one of those relationships last long term. I have coached many couples who were once just best friends counseling each other through their relationships. Then, after multiple relationships failed, they decided to give each other a try, and it always seemed to be a disaster. In a lot of cases, the man gets the woman, and then he realizes she isn't the goddess he made her out to be in his mind. He's built the sex up in his mind for so long that there's no way she can live up to it in reality. They get together and realize that dumping gossip on each other as friends is totally different from living together and being in a married relationship. Now they lose another relationship and also a friend. Their friendship got out of bounds and cost them greatly. I see it over and over. They didn't realize that one of the main reasons their other relationships failed was because they had each other. They were so focused on remaining friends and confiding in each other instead of their partners. They couldn't build anything real and sustainable with the people they dated because secretly they had been dating each other as friends all along. There was a protection mechanism in place and also a certain level of jealousy. They confided in each other, but the advice they gave was biased because neither of them really wanted to see the other person happily in love. It's a slippery slope.

Do you have friendships that are out of bounds? Is there a possibility a friend could be attracted to you? Is the advice you're receiving unbiased? Be honest with yourself first. Then move forward according to the truth.

Although I'm referring mainly to friends of the opposite sex, to have a friend of the same sex who is unhappy in his or her own life could be just as dangerous. You have to evaluate your girlfriends or your guy friends and ask them if they want to be in love and live happily with their spouse until the end of time. See if they are happy at work and in their current station in life. If the answer is no, you have to take them with a grain of salt. A negative friend with bad energy can affect your relationship in ways that will lead to a breakup. Remember, you must check your friends and make sure they truly want the best for you. You have a meter within your brain that helps you judge the advice you're receiving. Don't fool yourself or lie to yourself when you know the truth of the matter.

Cut off any inappropriate friendships, and give your relationship a fighting chance. Don't play with the Devil and expect him to play nicely. Be wise about your associations, and don't tempt yourself. You can't play with fire and not be burned. I know you want to trust yourself and you believe that you have it all under control, but you're still human. At the wrong time and in the wrong place, you can fall to your fleshly desires and lose it all. Be wise and keep the fight alive. Make your relationship work by focusing on home and not letting temptation get in the way.

Here are some things to think about:

1. Have you ever had to let a friend go for your relationship? If so, do you regret it?

2. If you felt suspicious of your spouse's friend, would you ask that the friend be removed? Why or why not?

3. Do you believe that certain friendships can ruin relationships? If not, why not?

4. Do you feel there is anyone you should put before your spouse?

5. Do you feel your loyalty should lie with your friend if you knew him or her before your spouse? Why or why not?

6. If your friend threatened to cut you off for being with your spouse, would you leave your spouse? Why or why not?

7. A friendship should be beneficial, not detrimental.

8. If your spouse doesn't agree with the friendship, let it go.

9. If your friends don't know your spouse, they aren't true friends.

10. Ask yourself why you're fighting for a friendship more than your relationship.

twenty-two

KEEP IT HOT

Never let your relationship get stale. If you feel like you're running out of love, start over and build love again. Don't ever get comfortable in your relationship to the point that you stop trying to please and impress your spouse. Many people will tell you that it's natural to get stagnant and that the fire will stop burning, but that does not have to be the case. If you notice that is the case for a season, do something about it. Don't let the world beat up on you. Don't lose the battle of love.

There are ways to keep your relationship hot, and you have to be open to trying new things. Be creative and fun. It may sound ridiculous at first, but do it anyway.

+ **Write love notes.** Take it back to high school, and take the time to write out your feelings on paper. My wife just did this for me, and it really touched my heart in a way a store-bought card can't.

✦ **Date every week.** Make sure you make time to date. Never stop dating. There are couples who aren't married yet and have already stopped dating. Get out of the house and do something that will set your senses on fire. Go skating if you can. Go bowling if you can. Go skydiving if you can. Go walk around the park or community lake. If you don't have any money to spend, then just spend time together.

✦ **Keep touching.** Always give a massage in the store or at night before you fall asleep. It may be only three minutes, but the touch means something. Hold hands when you're out and about. Give the other person a gentle rub as you pass by each other in the home. Stop and hug for a long minute or two. Keep kissing every chance you get.

✦ **Focus on the sexy.** There is something sexy about your spouse. Focus on that. Focus on it daily. If it's something tangible, stare at him or her for a minute or two. Just sit and admire. If it's their voice, remind yourself of the way it made you feel on the long phone calls you used to share. If it's their mind, sit and have a deep thirty-minute conversation every day.

✦ **Be spontaneous.** Go crazy in this area. There are so many things you can do to be spontaneous. It doesn't always have to be sex, although that can definitely be one of them. Whisk your spouse away for a one-night hotel stay. Call off work sick together, and spend the day doing what you both love to do. Pull an all-nighter watching movies, and get a sitter for the kids. Do what you hate to do but what your spouse loves to do. Show your love by getting out of your comfort zone for the other person, and make it a random act.

✦ **Send video texts instead of written texts.** Let your face be seen. It's so common to text nowadays. Instead of texting something flirty, say it on video and send it.

✦ **Create a love schedule.** You schedule meetings, workouts, hair appointments, and everything else. Why not put acts of love on the calendar? Remind yourself until it's second nature. Monday is foot rub night. Wednesday is the night you do their chores. Friday is back rub night. Sunday is breakfast in bed day.

Keep it hot, and keep it fresh! There is always something your mind can get into if you really think about it and get creative. Don't allow your relationship to fizzle out because you're complacent. Love should never be complacent.

If you get too comfortable and complacent, you will get replaced by something. I know that sounds a little harsh, but at some point it will come true. It is natural for the butterflies to go away. You will feel like you have done it all and said it all. Say it and do it over and over again, but find a different way.

You may get to a point where you feel you've put in enough work to last you a lifetime. That is why relationships go south. Love is a job with no retirement. You can't coast in love. With matters of the heart, you have to get up every day and go to work. If you don't work it, it won't work. Don't ever feel like you've arrived. So many of us have been guilty of this. It's human nature. You have to be mindful of this truth and do everything you can to combat it.

What you feed is what will grow. If you're feeding complacency, it will grow. If you're feeding arguments, they will grow. If you're feeding love, it will become stronger. Work for the results you want to generate. You would be surprised by how much a love schedule will help you. Set aside a time every day to focus completely on your spouse. Use this time to have in-depth conversations. If you can talk for an hour every day, then do so. If you can afford only thirty minutes, start there. I have seen relationships grow tremendously just by putting quality time on the calendar every day. You can't help but grow closer and strengthen your bond when you invest the time. Learn with every conversation. Pay attention to where the conversation goes left. Listen to the cues. Don't miss your opportunity to avoid an unnecessary argument. Don't get caught up in the routine of running your relationship into the ground. Focus on growth with every interaction. It is tedious at times. It will be painful to discipline yourself and to grow in your weak areas, but it's important to push yourself to that point.

There will be a moment in your relationship when you can choose to let it go or to push through. Don't miss the opportunity to move ahead and build even stronger. One of the most beautiful things my wife and I love to see is an elderly couple holding hands in public. It makes me wonder how they made it so far. I wonder how they even want to still touch each other after so many years. Then it hits me. I made the same choice. I decided to love my wife forever. I decided to sidestep the power struggles, avoid the unnecessary arguments, and strive for real love. I realized that after you get out of your way and you start to do what's best for love, everything changes. If you're being selfish, the relationship will not last. But when love is the focus and the goal, with every passing day, it gets stronger. I fall deeper in love by the day because I'm focused on loving, not fighting. I love my wife more today than I ever did, and we have been in this together more than a decade. It still feels new many days. I still get excited on date night. I didn't think it was possible to feel this way this far in, but now I know it's all based on how much you want it to work.

acknowledgments

First, I'd like to let you know that God is real. If you've wondered or doubted, please let me be a witness and testify to the authenticity of the divine power we know as God. I know there is a God of this universe because I would not be who I am without Him. I also thank Him for sending His son, Jesus, as an example and a savior. That gift changed my life. Every day I strive to be more like Christ.

I'd like to acknowledge my wife for not compromising her standards. Your self-love pushed me to learn how to love myself. It takes two to make it work, and you're the reason we're going on twelve years of marriage.

I'd like to thank my sons, Tony and Tayden, for putting a smile on my face every day and for being the reasons I continue in my purpose. I do not know the man I'd be had it not been for God blessing me with you two boys!

I'd like to thank my dad for setting an example for me to follow.

Had you not accepted your responsibilities, I probably would not have accepted mine. Thank you for showing me how to be a man.

I'd like to thank my mother for being the voice of encouragement. You always said, "Baby, you should be writing for a living." Well, Momma, I made it.

Thank you to my friends and family: Tesha, Miah, Liyah, Allen, Mrs. Elaine, Russ, Joe, and everyone else who has inspired me along the way.

Last but not least, I'd like to thank Latoya Smith, my literary agent, and Becky Nesbitt, my editor-at-large at Howard Books. Latoya, thank you for letting me know I could publish at this level and for being there when I decided I was ready. Becky, thank you for believing in the message. Your enthusiasm inspired me, and I know the connection was divine. I pray we can do many more books together.